Little Criminals

Dennis Foon has dedicated his career to creating thought-provoking and energetic dramas for children and young adults. Labelled as "unquestionably Canada's best young people's playwright" by Children's Literature Journal, Dennis Foon's most recent play, the acclaimed *The Short Tree and the Bird that Could Not Sing*, won the Chalmers Award in 1995 and has been heralded as one of his finest. His other plays include *Invisible Kids* (British Theatre Award), *Seesaw* (Our Choice Book Selection), *Skin* (Chalmers Award and Governor-General's Finalist), *New Canadian Kid, Liars, Mirror Game*, and the co-authored *Feeling Yes, Feeling No*. Dennis was a co-founder of Vancouver's Green Thumb Theatre where he was Artistic Director from 1975 to 1987. His work in television and film includes *Maggie's Secret* for CBS (Scott Newman Award), his adaptation of *Skin* (Gold Medal, New York International TV Festival; Gemini Nominee) and numerous scripts for episodic television.

Little Criminals

by
Dennis Foon

Blizzard Publishing • Winnipeg

Little Criminals first published 1996 by
Blizzard Publishing Inc.
73 Furby Street, Winnipeg, Canada R3C 2A2
© 1996 Dennis Foon

Images from the film *Little Criminals* used by
permission of the CBC.
Storyboards © Kelly Brine used with permission.
Printed in Canada by Friesens Printing Ltd.

Published with the assistance of
the Canada Council and the Manitoba Arts Council.

Canadian Cataloguing in Publication Data

Foon, Dennis, 1951–
  Little Criminals
  ISBN 0-921368-62-3
I. Title.
PS8561.062L58 1996 C812'.54 C96-920003-X
PR9199.3.F5667L58 1996

Contents

Foreword

by Brian Freeman

There is a truism about narrative fiction which holds that to find a story worth telling is the easy part; the hard part is to find the way of the telling. The process of wayfinding is rarely self-evident and in no narrative art is that more the normal state of affairs than in the art of screenwriting. For the writer of screenplays, the real job is found in the often interminable process of re-writing. Given the complexities of the media of film and television, their rich and fast-evolving vocabularies, and the universal "literacy" of film and television audiences, that is hardly surprising.

Audiences must be seduced and challenged at the same time. How to enchant and provoke using highly familiar vocabulary—that's the trick. And if the seduction and the challenge are not in some kind of dynamic balance, one's hold on an audience is jeopardized: they tune out. The story must seem to unfold naturally yet be full of a thousand calculations all driven by the knowledge that time is running out (the vicissitudes of TV scheduling enforce that) and, perhaps more crucially, so is the attention span of the average viewer.

What is surprising is that once in a very long while a great screenplay will emerge from the raw story material in quite short order. Such a one is Dennis Foon's script for *Little Criminals*, which went from research phase to production script in a little over a year. Mr Foon is an assiduous researcher, and the fact that he knew the subject of under-aged kids in crime so well undoubtedly played a part in getting the story camera-ready so quickly. Another major factor had to be the central characters of the story, who vividly declared their ownership of the narrative quite early on. Vicious and vulnerable eleven-year old Des is to my mind as compelling a creation in his own way as Truffault's Doisnel in his classic tale of juvenile crime, *Four Hundred Blows*.

If *Little Criminals* is long-form television drama at its most challenging, it is also ninety-plus minutes of gripping entertainment. CBC Television is proud of its role in developing and producing this feature length drama.

Brian Freeman is Executive Director in Charge of Development,
Movies and Mini-Series, at CBC Television.

Producer's Note

Though I'm sure no film is easy to produce, *Little Criminals* presented a very particular set of difficulties, especially in approaching it as a movie for television. As a "hot topic," the project had obvious appeal, but it was clear from the very early stages that the film had to be relentless in its honesty, that it would demand darkness and edginess as its watchwords, that there was no comfort to be found in the material, no simple resolution to the problems it explored. These are not always the prime categories for getting material to broadcast. Fortunately, in the CBC, we had a network who not only encouraged this approach, but actually demanded it. But when we emerged with first the script and then the film, we all had to take a long look at what we had created. Discussions of levels of "responsible broadcasting," public acceptability to language and depiction of violence went on at every stage of production.

Ultimately, though, the same responsibility that guided first the writing then the shooting of the movie demanded that we not pull back, that we not compromise the integrity of the project. The result is a movie that is disturbing on a lot of levels. But it is more disturbing to me that people thought we were making this stuff up, that we were exaggerating and sensationalizing the issue. That people thought and could continue to think that "it can't happen here."

This film is for adults to reflect on the society that we have created, for parents who are worried about who their children are or might become, and for kids to understand the consequences of their actions. And to those who would say that our film is too violent, too explicit to be suitable for young audiences, I can only wish that instead of putting their efforts into protecting our children from the images of *Little Criminals* they would spend their energy protecting our children from the reality.

—Phil Savath

Screenwriter's Note

While researching a play in Winnipeg, I met a few pre-pubescent kids who were heavily involved in criminal activities. One of the boys, eleven, had recently been busted doing a B&E with a friend and his three-year-old sister. He said he was baby-sitting.

I was bewildered by this encounter, wanted to know more. I wondered what forces shaped kids like this, what if anything could be done for them. I was curious to know if these kids were unique or if more was going on than I suspected.

In the spring of 1993, I gave a two page proposal to Susan Duligal (at the time an executive at CBC Drama). The tale I had in mind was "of two friends, both young thugs, who live very, very close to the edge ... one of the boys will go off the deep end, cost a life and probably lose his own. The other boy will have some kind of lifeline —that one person who is there for him, on some level, the one who pulls him through."

At the time, I asked CBC to simply fund an initial stage of research. I wanted to find out how real this situation was in Canada—and to see if the thread of a story I had in mind could be realistically fleshed out. Susan took it to Jim Burt, Head of Movies and Mini-Series, who gave me total support. His only request was that I be completely truthful in the telling. I was to pull no punches. For this directive I was extraordinarily grateful, for within hours of beginning my research, I realized just how deep and disturbing this material was.

I spent months interviewing social workers, youth workers, psychologists, teachers. In three cities: Toronto, Vancouver, and Winnipeg. Spoke to hundreds of kids, some in school, some in care, some just picked up by the cops. I spent a lot of time with the police. Hanging out with school liaison officers. Going on drive-alongs with the youth squad.

It rapidly became apparent that the incidents I had first heard about in Winnipeg were anything but unique; they were simply the tip of the iceburg. The events I ultimately used in the screenplay were occurrences that were recounted to me again and again by professionals working across the country.

Eventually I wrote a storyline, creating the character of Des as a synthesis of several tales I heard of ten- or eleven-year-olds who ran their own gangs. This storyline was very much the template for what finally became the movie. The central question: Is Des a criminal or a victim? The answer: Both—but he was a victim first.

After presenting the storyline to CBC, Jim asked me to go to outline and screenplay and to pick a producer/story editor to work with. To me, the choice was obvious—Phil Savath, who I had known for many years and worked with extensively the last few. I had deep respect for both his abilities and his integrity and knew that with a project like this, those qualities would be crucial. His effectiveness was immeasurably complemented by the addition of Brian Freeman to the team. As the CBC executive in charge, Brian ensured that things went smoothly and he continued to protect the development process.

From that point on, things went very quickly. The outline was finished in Spring of 1994. The first draft was completed that summer. We then approached Steven Surjik to direct. He received it before getting on a plane to Toronto. When he got off, he left an incredibly long message on my machine, which was a writer's dream; he loved the first draft, and just wanted to shoot it the way it was. In fact, what he filmed was very close to the original script, richly amplified by his passion and vision.

This project was blessed by an enormously talented production team who shared a belief. They felt this story reflected a reality that needed to be seen, and they used every drop of their artistry and energy to make it happen. When a group of artists is that ardent and unified, the result is exhilarating and has a reasonable chance to touch others.

—Dennis Foon

Interview with the Director

Gerald L'Ecuyer: Talk to me about the actual physical setting, where you were when you first cracked open the script. Where, what, how?

Stephen Surjik: I was working in pre-production for an episode of *The X-Files*. I was in the Sutton Place Hotel, living in a room there. The phone rang and it was Phil Savath, actually a message from Phil Savath, regarding a script he wanted me to read. That was the first I'd heard of it. He shipped the script over, I read the first page, and I was absolutely intrigued.

GL: By what?

SS: The reality of the script, the verisimilitude of the language, and by the harshness of the language in context of the characters. The narrative is almost entirely from the point of view of Des, the key character. The other thing that I liked immensely was the very nihilistic, well-observed pathology of this kid's spiral downwards.

GL: So you sort of locked into this kid, right away.

SS: Instantly understood him. Or understood the script which explains him. And maybe understood him.

GL: There's an other-worldly quality, from the very beginning, a sense of timelessness that I picked up when I watched the final result. How did that manifest itself from script to screen?

SS: First of all I think that style answers script. Style is born from the script. The style we chose to go with was the subjective perspective of the main character. So it began in the script, where you have a character on a page, and almost everything is observed from his point of view. And we followed that in terms of the style of our shooting. We tried to shoot it following Des around without him

Gerald L'Ecuyer conducted this interview with Stephen Surjik, the director of *Little Criminals,* in Toronto on August 21, 1995. L'Ecuyer is a filmmaker and journalist and is currently working for BRAVO!

11

catching us following him. We shot it from his height physically. We shot it with lenses that were very subjective focal lengths. We cast all the other characters as being seen from this young man's point of view, this young child who is all of eleven years old. So everybody he sees is a bit goofy, is a bit false, is a bit inauthentic. It helps alienate his character that way.

GL: The way Des is written, what connected with you as a person?

SS: Well I think that there is an aspect of Des that is extremely destructive, the character is on this spiral downwards. I think that all people are kind of fascinated with car accidents when they drive by, they want to look. So there was certainly that voyeuristic aspect that I was interested in. As a young boy myself, I got into just a little bit of trouble; small time arson, small time hood, very small time. But, what attracted me as a kid to that whole environment was just the excitement of it all, it was simply fun. You break a window, your heart gets pumping and you run away and that's exciting. That's not based upon wanting to get back at anybody or a broken family or a society which has let you down. It's not a victim driven thing. It's just a very pure look at the motive, the beginnings of that kind of trouble.

GL: Right. But in a sense, in this movie though, Des is let down by a lot of people.

SS: Absolutely. Des does not have a family that's effective at all in being able to catch him, keep him from going through the cracks, whereas the other boy, his friend Cory, has a family that is kinda messed up but they still catch him and they do not, they will not, let him fall, they hold on to him. Des's family does not make the catch, and that's why he goes all the way, he goes right through and it becomes a tragedy. I think that a lot of boys have that inclination. The difference between the two lead characters, Cory and Des, is that Cory has a family and Des does not.

GL: Dennis Foon created Des for the page, so when you read the character how did you sort out what your obligations were in terms of Des?

SS: Well, a very good question, but very complex. I used to think, for instance, that the script was the most important thing when you're making a dramatic show. Now, I actually think the actor is the most important thing because people are more interested—I'm more interested—in watching somebody who is engaging and interesting do ... whatever. You get a great script and you don't have a good actor, it's uninteresting. And yet I loved the script that Dennis produced and set up, so the challenge was to find somebody that was at least as good as the script. When I look for an actor that can play eleven years old, or any actor for that matter, I am looking for somebody that can both interpret the material in the moment, that is, just make it real, and I'm looking for somebody who can take my direction, my interpretation of the material—someone who can equally synthesize these two things and make it happen live. It is a tremendously difficult job, there's nobody in the world that can do it and if you find somebody who is vaguely appropriate, well then you're laughing. We were extremely fortunate because we found two young actors, Miles Ferguson and Brendan Fletcher, who play Cory and Des respectively, and they are both truly great actors.

GL: It seems to me even in his personality, and in his roles as an actor and as a character, Brendan has a profound understanding.

SS: You know, he is an ancient soul in a very young body. His clarity and understanding of the world is magnificent. There is such a ridiculous level of nuance that went on in this whole thing that it's difficult to nail down one specific example. I can give you an example of his power as an actor. I was lensing up a very dry rehearsal of a scene where his mother accidentally cuts him. We were going to walk through by the numbers and see this thing play. In the shot, he's in the doorway, hiding behind a crack in the door. So I went behind the door to watch the scene from his point of view because, as I said earlier, I was trying to play everything essentially from his perspective. The actors started walking the lines and I was watching through the little crack in the door and I could hear somebody sniffling in the corner and I looked over and it was Brendan and he was crying. I asked him what was wrong and he said "we're rehearsing aren't we?" I said, "Yeah we are rehearsing but it is very important that you—" of course you see, what's happening on the other side of the door is very traumatic for his character and so I suggested that he retain his emotional epiphanies because it was going to be a long day. It was going to be a long time before he was going to be on camera. He said no, no, he had to get into it and he had to support the other actors so that they knew someone was behind the door. We went through that scene a dozen times and a dozen times he wept like a little boy, a dozen times he had an entire emotional breakdown and he would just keep doing it and simply refused to let me kinda hold him back. And it had a tremendous effect on all the other actors.

GL: So, let's go back to the content of the script. We've got a character who doesn't seem to have a chance from the get go.

SS: Right.

GL: And he continues to sink deeper and deeper into something. As I was watching it I kept waiting for the happy ending, hoping that somehow people are going to help him. Talk about that aspect of it ... I was torn when I was watching it because I kept hoping, or maybe I'm just very familiar with seeing the opposite: oh, troubled kid, and here's the solution.

SS: I think that if we had attempted to give it a happy ending it simply wouldn't have been real ... or well observed. It wouldn't have been a true rendition of the situation. It is a tragedy and it is sad and it doesn't propose a lot of answers. I think there are answers there, I think there are solutions. But, they certainly can't be dealt with in fifteen seconds on a news blip or some TV movie.

GL: But then whenever there's a monster in a society, whether it be a child who is irredeemable or whatever, it seems to reflect society as a whole. It's about ourselves because if there is a person out there who is so troubled, and so unable to be helped, it does say something about our own lives. Is that something you were conscious of during the production?

SS: When I was a kid, in school, I was always the class clown's best friend, I was always the kid that sort of egged him on and got him in trouble. I was always there. I was the witness. I was his enabler, his audience, and the odd thing about it is that, in the case of Cory, he's Des's enabler. At the end, when he backs out, he backs away from Des, and Des has nothing left because that's the only thing he had. It's a story about a relationship between two guys, it's a love story in many ways, how one of them gets freaked out, and the other backs away and causes a schism that is insurmountable.

GL: Right. Let's talk about some of the production quibbles. The first one being why and how the CBC accepted it. Reading the script anyone would know they are getting into some really adult material, some pretty racey material.

SS: Yeah they did. Phyllis Platt actually saw the proposal for the development process and she agreed, she wanted to see this film made, and she pushed it all along to get it made. I kept asking them whether or not they wanted to make this film because it would be quite coarse, a very harsh snapshot of reality. I also wanted to make sure that it was going to be fun, from the kids' point of view, it would be a very fun thing for the first six acts; they're having a good time. All the violence, all the damage was all just a good time for them. I wanted to make it a good time for the audience. I wanted them to enjoy that process, I wanted them to get sucked in. I didn't want it to be just a third person snapshot of these monsters. I wanted the audience to be a member of the gang.

GL: Right.

SS: So, logistically, the making of the film was tremendously difficult because we were dealing with a bunch of minors, ten- and eleven-year-old boys, a three-year-old girl. They had to smoke cigarettes, they had to drive their cars on the street, they had to drive motorcycles without helmets, they had to do dangerous stuff and do very difficult emotional stuff all the time and it was just a tremendously demanding and extremely nerve-racking shooting process. We wanted to keep everyone safe and we didn't want to risk anything, and everyone was always nervous about that, especially myself.

GL: How did you talk to the kids about the language and about what they were doing?

SS: Well, we tried to involve their parents as much as we could. There were no surprises when the kids went home. The parents were extremely supportive and they were all involved in the making of the movie. We had to spend a lot of time in rehearsal, and we were short on rehearsal time and the CBC sprung for another week which absolutely saved us.

GL: What was Dennis's take on the production as he saw his script come to life?

SS: I'm always nervous when the writer comes on set because I'm afraid that I'm not doing justice to what he or she has done. I feel terribly guilty immediately if I have wavered from the text anywhere, but I didn't really. There were one or two occasions where it got away from me, it was certainly not something I was in the habit of doing. Dennis seemed quite excited as it started to come together bit by bit. We had a great working relationship. I'd always ask him about stuff that I wanted to change, if I needed to change it. Totally, totally open minded about everything.

GL: What would he be sorry about if it wasn't there?

SS: I've never asked him that general a question about such a specific subject but I thought that he, like I, was most elated to see the boys' relationship on screen and to see that come to life. I think that was probably the thing that we were most worried about.

GL: And also you don't want to tangle with the hurdles that he had to go through in the creation of the script. Those hurdles are his; you don't want to mesh your hurdles with his, or get into his …

SS: That's his luggage, I've got my own problems. I would often go to him with my problems, to have him solve them and he would, and Phil Savath as well, we would all solve them. Phil is a writer too, and so it was interesting to see Phil work as a producer because he really understood. As a writer and producer he understands a small thing that is on the page, how important it is to get it on the screen even though it might be like the kids throwing bulbs at the car and then them driving off. That takes like a minute and a half on screen and of course it took us two days to shoot.

GL: And, how do you feel about people who may look at the film and say, "My god this is just violence, violence, violence," seemingly, absolutely without hope.

SS: I think that the film is certainly violent but it goes somewhere. There is a moment when you think that this kid is going to find that he has caught onto something and he is going to get help and he's going to make good and get out of his predicament and then he slips and he falls all the way down.

GL: Very often it happens like that in life, right? Very often there is no rescue. I know that for a fact, as a human. The hardest part watching the film was that it really does remind me that at times in life there is no rescue, and this kid is never rescued in a way. The adults try to help him but ultimately he doesn't have a chance, it's like he's never had a chance.

SS: Des's downfall is ultimately his only weakness. He goes back to get that stupid monkey that the girl leaves in the house. That's when he gets arrested. He gets arrested, he gets caught and that whole thing starts because of a weakness in himself for other people.

GL: Is it a weakness or was it an act of generosity?

SS: Well, yeah, it could certainly be seen as an act of generosity. But, in that scenerio where they've just broken into a place and left, it would be … it could be even considered as an act of stupidity to go back. *(Laughs.)* He feels bad for the little girl and yes, it's an act of generosity, and it's an act of courage and it's an act of weakness as well. It's a lot of different things and that's why he falters, in that moment he is caring for other people.

GL: It's pretty bleak. Even this act of caring and humanity, ironically, it ends up being a—

SS: —a downfall.

GL: Yeah. But, this is a bit of an antithesis to what people are used to seeing, because they usually see the happy ending or even the happy-but-a-little-sad ending.

SS: Yeah. It's certainly unusual for me to do that on a commercial level.

GL: It will attract a lot of people but it will also affect a lot of people.

SS: Well, I think it's a very compelling story and I think it's a very sad story and I've never ever done a show before where someone's been shot. I've never done a movie or a show where there has been a gun in it, or a drink in it, or they smoked. I'm very conscious about the kind of material that I do because I don't want to donate anymore poison to an already screwed up television system. It's hugely influential on people. *Wayne's World 2* was a movie about adults for kids, this is a movie about kids for adults.

Little Criminals

A *note on this script*

This is not the production script. There are a few differences between this published screenplay and what was actually included in the final cut of the film. The production script is written in nine acts to conform with CBC's requirements for commercial breaks. The act endings were at the finish of scenes: 19, 28, 38, 42, 59, 67, 83, 88, and 101.

I have also included in this draft a few scenes and moments that did not make it into the final cut, principally due to the tight time restrictions of network television. While I am certain their omission did not compromise the film, I thought these sequences would be of interest to the reader. Included here are scene 43, Des being driven home by the police, and scene 44, when they bring him home and meet his grandmother. I've also left in a voice-over in scene 63.

—Dennis Foon

1. Interior. Examination Room. Video Image.

Portions of interviews with DES at the Children's House are interspersed throughout the film.

DES, a pale blond-haired eleven-year-old, rocks in his chair, looking at his feet. After a moment, he lifts his head and stares straight at us.

Fade in:

> DES
> Hello. Fuck you.

The image flickers out and we're in ...

2. Interior. An Old Building. Dusk.

Small hands pull on the glowing four-foot tube of a grimy fluorescent fixture. The flickering fluorescent glow reveals the face of DES, a bit dirtier and wilder than in the previous shot.

Perched on the hulking shoulders of STACKER, another kid, DES yanks the bulb free and the dying light plunges the decaying building into darkness.

Begin Titles.

3. Exterior. A Lonely Corner. Dusk.

A "Don't Walk" sign flashes, reflecting on a drizzly Vancouver street corner.

Ignoring its warning, a small hooded figure darts across the intersection on a collision course with a brand new Lexus.

At the last second, the sedan skids to a stop, apparently knocking the child over.

The worried DRIVER, a fortyish business guy, leaps out of the car.

DRIVER
Oh, my god ...

*But the boy, unhurt, pops up. It's DES. He gives the amazed
DRIVER the finger, spits on the windshield and jumps up and down
on the hood. The DRIVER, stunned, stares at him. And DES runs off
laughing.*

DRIVER
(as the adrenaline hits)
You little bastard!

*He looks around and sees DES lingering by the entrance of a
parking structure. He jumps back behind the wheel and squeals off
after DES, who disappears into the shadows of the parkade. The
car follows.*

4. Interior. Parkade. Dusk.

The Lexus cruises through the underlit concrete, hunting.

DRIVER's P.O.V.

*As the car descends another level, the headlights pick up the sil-
houette of DES, his back to the car.*

DRIVER
(under his breath)
Gotcha.

*He speeds up, then screeches to a halt inches from the kid. DES
slowly turns, smirking. He's holding a four-foot fluorescent tube.
Menacingly, he lifts it.*

*Behind DES, five more children appear out of nowhere (mixed
race: the youngest is MOUSE, eight, the oldest is the hulking
STACKER, twelve). They all hold fluorescent tubes. Then raise
them over their heads.*

On the wide-eyed driver:

As the tubes smash against the car.

*An explosion of shattering glass bursts against the windshield like
hailstones, the kids breaking tube after tube, a blizzard of shrapnel.*

*The DRIVER, panicking, floors it in reverse, and slams into a
concrete pillar. The car alarm starts to wail. The dazed business-
man emerges from the car only to have DES and crew descend on
him. MOUSE gleefully lifts his wallet and hands it to DES.*

Suddenly, they hear a strange, high-pitched whistle and stop.

TAK, ten, the whistler, is the eyes of the gang who, if he does speak, never does it in the group. He points. DES looks.

A SECURITY GUARD is charging straight for DES.

> DES
> *(to his crew)*
> History.

Protecting his leader, STACKER throws himself in front of the GUARD, toppling him. The kids wildly break for it, leaping over the downed GUARD on the way. But he manages to hang onto the squirming STACKER.

> MOUSE
> Stacker!

DES has a quick look back. The other kids eye him. DES pulls the cash out of the guy's wallet.

> DES
> We roll.

He throws the wallet and takes off, the kids whooping behind him.

End titles.

Dissolve to:

5. Interior. Video Store. Dusk.

On the monitor, Christopher the Christmas Tree is singing with his forest friends.

CORY, a dark, angel-faced boy, tall for his eleven years, stares blankly at the kiddy show. VINCE, thirties, pockmarked faced and a bit of a pot, nudges him.

> VINCE
> Find something yet?

> CORY
> *(holding up a Steven Seagal video)*
> This one.

> VINCE
> Come on, man, your little sister's gotta watch it too.

> CORY
> What sister?

VINCE winces, but won't bite.

> VINCE
> Just keep looking, Cory, will ya?

> CORY
> I looked. Just get what you want. That's what
> you were gonna do anyway.

And CORY abruptly leaves.

> VINCE
> Cory, come on—

But he's gone. VINCE, frustrated, watches his stepson shove through the exit. He just can't get it right with this kid.

6. Exterior. Video Store. Night.

CORY stands outside the entrance, impatiently waiting for VINCE. In the distance, he hears a loud "Whoop!" and looks.

The street lamps project the shadows of DES and his pals. They're still on a manic roll, running on top of the cars parked on the side street. Leaping from the hood of one car to the trunk of the next, up the roof and down again, trashing paint jobs.

CORY watches these locusts swarm toward him with interest. Finally they arrive at a carpet-cleaning truck a little distance from CORY. DES, flanked by the entire gang, sizes up CORY. CORY doesn't blink at the six menacing faces. DES holds out his hand. NICK, ten, places a spark plug in it. DES twists it, breaking off the porcelain tip. Then he bobs it in his palm for CORY's benefit. DES whirls, hurling it into the truck's side window, crystallizing the glass. He checks back with CORY, challenging him to do something. But CORY simply shrugs: he couldn't give a shit.

TAK whistles. DES smiles and slinks off, followed by the others just as VINCE charges out of the video store.

> VINCE
> Hey!

But the kids are history. VINCE checks the smashed glass on his truck.

> VINCE
> Did you see that? Did you see them do this?

CORY just looks at him. VINCE lets out the sigh of a parent in a losing relationship, then shoves his elbow against the shattered window.

7. Exterior. Chet's House. Dusk.

DES and his pals clamber up the rotting steps of a weedy east-side duplex. Broken bottles and trash decorate the neighbourhood. JAMAL, eleven, swaggers up to the door past DES, assuming STACKER's usual position. DES shoves him off the top step. JAMAL careens into NICK, and the two crash on the ground. The others cautiously observe.

> JAMAL
> What was that for?

> DES
> Practice.

JAMAL, physically much bigger than DES, is seething: this isn't the end of it.

DES pounds on the door. It slowly opens. CHET leans on the threshold, a mean-looking post-grunge seventeen-year-old. He's holding a half-eaten carton of Chinese food. Vintage headbanger metal blares from inside where a perpetual party's going down; CHET shares this place with four or five other rowdy guys.

> CHET
> Hey, it's Des and the midget army.

> DES
> Whatcha got?

CHET hands DES his container of food. Then picks up a baggie of joints and gives it to DES.

> CHET
> For you.

DES hands him the carton of food back.

> DES
> For you.

> CHET
> C'mon, cough it up.

DES pulls out his roll of bills and gives him a few.

> CHET
> Not enough.

                         DES
              It was enough yesterday.
                        CHET
              Yesterday you had backup. Today ...

CHET nods disparagingly at the gang. DES, fuming, takes out the roll. Pulls out a fiver.

                        CHET
              I'll take that one too.

CHET reaches over and takes another, leaving DES with a twenty and change.

                        CHET
              Just business, huh?
                         DES
                      (pissed off)
              Whatever.
                        CHET
              Hey! No hard feelings, okay? Alright? Look,
              alright, I'll give you's a bonus.

CHET reaches in his pocket. Pulls out a four inch square sheet of paper with a half dozen red dots on it.

                        CHET
              Mind Candy.

He drops it into DES's palm.

                        CHET
              Have a nice flight.

CHET closes the door. The kids go.

                        JAMAL
              That guy's a rip-off.
                         DES
              Like you know.

MOUSE, very small and baby faced, runs up to DES. He's followed by SAM, eight, a middle-class kid.

                        MOUSE
              What'd ya get?
                         DES
              Lick 'm Ups. Want some?

SAM
Yeah!

JAMAL
He wouldn't rip you like that if Stacker was
standin' here.

DES
Chet gets what I give him.

JAMAL
This stuff could be rat poison.

DES
So?

DES licks it.

8. Exterior. Empty Downtown East-side Street. Night.

A flame shoots up in the air.

MOUSE, on top of a toppled mailbox, squirts flame with a can of lighter fluid. Some of the fire splashes near JAMAL.

Running at MOUSE full force, JAMAL sends him flying. MOUSE manages to land on his feet. SAM screeches with laughter. The boys are very stoned.

DES grabs the lighter fluid, ignites the top of the can, and drops it in.

DES
I hate junk mail.

The kids all watch expectantly ... BOOM! Mail and bits of mailbox fill the air. And they run.

9. Interior. Classroom. Day.

DES sits at his desk, drawing an intricate jungle scene into the pages of his textbook. A tiger's red eyes peek menacingly through the equations.

The TEACHER, a blur, is at the blackboard, back to the class, trying to teach something about math.

TEACHER
... times three equals thirty three. Now you
look to see where to put the parenthesis ...

As the teacher turns to the blackboard, there's a knock on the open door. Police CONSTABLE CLARKE, mid-forties, in uniform, amiably stands at the threshold. A knowing nod to the teacher. Who sighs.

TEACHER

Des.

Everybody watches as DES slowly rises. He likes the attention. As he saunters out, he and CORY share a look. CORY shakes his head. DES rolls his eyes.

10. Interior. Hallway. Day.

The instant DES is through the door, CLARKE corners him against the lockers. He's not touching the kid, but intimidation is his goal.

CLARKE

Last night was quite the party, Des. You gotta wise up, kid.

DES

What?

CLARKE

Last night.

DES

I was doing homework.

CLARKE

Right, ditto for your pal Stacker. Only he neglected to remember turning twelve last month. That's why he'll score six months in the slammer for the job.

DES smiles.

CLARKE

You're laughing now, Des boy, but come your twelfth birthday, I know ten cops who'll be at your door with the cake.

DES eyes CLARKE with an uncanny coldness.

DES

What if my buds and me jump you? Pour gas on you, burn your skin off. You only got six shots in that gun.

They stare at each other. The recess bell rings. Instantly the hall is filled with kids and CLARKE shakes his head as DES disappears in the tide.

11. Exterior. Monkey Bars. Day.

Kids swarm on the playground, doing the recess thing: tag, throwing balls, sharing snacks ... DES watches over the schoolyard like a warlord, covertly sharing a cigarette with the hollow-eyed TAK. DES spots CORY standing alone near the graffiti-covered school steps. TAK nudges DES.

MOUSE and SAM excitedly scoot up to DES. They're both holding sticks. JAMAL is right behind, dragging a pale, terrified nine-year-old to the king.

> MOUSE
> I found the Dink under the portable, Des.

> SAM
> I found him.

> MOUSE
> Shut up, I saw the Dink first.

> SAM
> Yeah, well I got the sticks.

MOUSE gives SAM a whack across the arm. DES goes to the kid they call the DINK.

> DES
> Hi Baby.

DES lights a wooden match and flicks it at him. The DINK squirms away.

> DES
> What did Mommy give you for me today?

The DINK produces a coin. MOUSE gives it to DES.

> DES
> That's it?

> JAMAL
> *(shaking the kid)*
> Is that it? Is that it?

DES holds out his hand. NICK puts a used syringe in his palm.

> DES
>
> Hey, look what I found.

He puts it up to the DINK's face. JAMAL smiles.

> DES
>
> You want it?
> *(putting the needle to the kid's throat)*
> Maybe it's got aids, whaddya think?
> *(off the kid's pleading look)*
> Five bucks tomorrow, right?

The DINK nods yes. MOUSE viciously jabs him with his stick.

> MOUSE
>
> Don't be a stranger.

DES's eyes follow the DINK as he runs off past a scuffle. He watches the fight with interest.

CORY is shoved by JOSH and a friend. CORY shoves back. Hard.

12. Exterior. Playground. Day. Continuing.

A crowd of kids is gathered around the fight. DES watches CORY being held by the friend as JOSH punches him in the stomach. CORY gives the friend an elbow and breaks free. He gives a quick backhand to JOSH. A few smacks and kicks and both are down. CORY's hardly out of breath. As the crowd breaks up, DES approaches CORY from behind and pats him on the shoulder.

> DES
>
> Hey—

CORY, thinking it's another attack, whirls and hits DES, knocking him to the ground. Looking, CORY realizes who he shoved. And stoically awaits his fate as DES slowly rises. They never take their eyes off each other. DES, expressionless, steps toward CORY. Reaches in his pocket. MOUSE and NICK share a nervous glance. A weapon? CORY braces himself. DES pulls out the bag he got from CHET. Smiles. Reaches in and gives CORY a joint.

> CORY
>
> ... What's that for?

> DES
>
> Victory.

DES walks. MOUSE runs up to him. DES magnanimously hands

him the bag. NICK grabs it from MOUSE. As NICK distributes the joints to the rest of the gang, DES saunters away. Top of the world.

13. Exterior. Des's House. Night.

East-side Vancouver, around Pandora Street, not far from the fish plants. This area is a mix of small, ancient warehouses and the odd decrepit house. The aging little place DES walks up to needs a paint job, new roof, new everything. No grass, just weeds. DES struts up to the door, feeling good. Tries the door. It's locked. Knocks. No answer. Harder. Listens. He hears a TV blasting inside. He jumps off the porch, running to a basement window. He opens it and crawls in.

14. Interior. Des's House/Hallway. Night.

The basement door opens, revealing DES. TV fills the house, it's a reality-based cop show. DES moves toward the sound.

15. Interior. Living room. Night.

DOLLY, a hard-looking woman in her forties, watches the cops cuff a killer, oblivious to DES. A younger woman in her mid-twenties, RUTH, is lying on the couch. Her face is bruised. DES sits beside her. She groggily opens her eyes.

> DES
> Hi, Mom.

> RUTH
> *(warmly)*
> Hey, Des, how you doin', honey?
> *(bellows)*
> Mom, turn that damn thing down!

DOLLY, without acknowledging RUTH or taking her eyes off the tube, lifts the remote and turns down the volume.

> DES
> Brought you something.

> RUTH
> Aw, whadja get me?

He pulls out a pack of cigarettes and the twenty-dollar bill.

> RUTH
> That's sweet, Des.

DES puts a cigarette in her mouth and lights it with his lighter.

> RUTH
> Supper's in the kitchen. Getcher self somethin'
> to eat.

DES heads into the kitchen.

16. Interior. Kitchen. Night.

The kitchen's messy but nothing a half day of scrubbing couldn't fix. Not a thing on the stove. DES checks the oven. Empty. DES opens the fridge. A dried out, half-eaten TV dinner, coffee cream, a murky jar of pickles. Nothing particularly edible. He opens the freezer door. Box of frozen popsicles. He takes one. From the living room he hears the sound of the TV being turned back up. He heads out.

He wanders back into the living room. RUTH is passed out again, DOLLY ignores him. DES, sucking his popsicle, stands behind her watching the screen. After a few seconds he takes the lit cigarette out of his mother's mouth, stubs it out and goes.

17. Interior. Des's Room. Night.

DES enters his room. Faded wallpaper, some ripped up posters on the walls. The floor is a swamp of dirty clothes, moldy dishes and garbage bags. There's a dirty sheet and blanket sprawled on the ancient mattress. DES opens the closet door. Goes in and closes the door behind him.

18. Interior. Des's Closet. Night.

DES turns on a big drycell flashlight. With a pen knife, he pulls up a floorboard. Lifts out an old metal box. Opens it. The box is filled with money, IDs, some bits of jewellery. DES adds what's left of his bank roll to the box. Takes out some marking pens. The closet walls are covered with his drawings, a collage of jumbled images: A cyborg blasting a rocket gun, a Tyrannosaurus Rex jawing a bit-off arm, an exploding head, swastikas ... and DES continues work on a half-finished drawing of a tiger with fangs dripping blood.

DES *(V.O.)*
People are always making up lies about me,
blaming everything on me, shoving me around.
It's not fair ...

19. Interior. Examination Room. Video Image.

DES (V.O.)
... Like with that guy in the parking lot, I
wasn't even there. I was home, helping my
mom. Ask her if you don't believe me.

20. Exterior. An East-end Street. Day. Next morning.

*CORY's walking alone, book bag slung over his shoulder. He looks
up as a motorcycle thunders down the street, gaining on him. The
Triumph skids to a halt in front of him. The biker rips his helmet off.
It's DES.*

DES
You fight good. Hear that's why you got kicked
out of your last school.

CORY
What's it to ya?

DES
Ever do anything else?

CORY
So what are you, king shit?

DES
That's right. Hop on.

CORY
This yours?

DES
Is now.

DES gives the starter a kick. Once. Twice. Finally it catches.

CORY
Ride to school?

DES
Screw school. I thought you wanted in.

CORY climbs on.

21. Interior. Army & Navy Department Store on Hastings Street. Day.

Through binoculars, we see the surveillance camera, the hardware section, the clothing area, an empty check out.

> SALESLADY *(off-screen)*:
> Shouldn't you boys be in school?

> DES *(off-screen)*:
> No, Missus, it's a Professional Development Day.

At the counter with the elderly SALESLADY as DES scopes the store with the Army Surplus binoculars.

> SALESLADY *(off-screen)*:
> I could use one of those. So how do you like 'em?

DES hands them back.

> DES
> Too heavy.
> *(eyeing the display behind her)*
> Maybe the ones over there.

> SALESLADY
> Which are you after?

She turns to look. Behind DES, CORY is nervously pocketing candy, hockey cards and a GI Joe-type action figure from the shelves.

> DES
> Not those, no the other ones. Yeah, the ones next to them ...

22. Interior. Another Part of the Store. Day.

CORY, pockets bulging, anxiously walks with DES toward the exit, past the tool section. Suddenly DES grabs a screwdriver off a shelf and pulls CORY over to an empty salesdesk and they both disappear.

Crouched below the unmanned cash register, DES unwraps the screwdriver.

> CORY
> What're you doin?

DES jimmies the drawer open. Reaches up, brings his hand back down and opens his palm: filled with sparkling quarters.

23. Exterior. The Docks. Day.

Scenic Vancouver: A blackened dock with a view of the brackish water, grimy freighters and mountains of yellow sulphur. In this PCB heaven, DES and CORY stuff their faces with candy while checking the booty.

> DES
> Your share.

He pulls a handful of change out of his pocket, slaps it on the gravel. Mostly pennies and nickels.

> CORY
> How come you get all that?

> DES
> You don't see me wasting time lifting baby toys.

He tosses the hockey cards to CORY.

> DES
> *(picks up the GI Joe)*
> What you gonna do with this crap?

He heaves it away. Then DES softens.

> DES
> *(intimately)*
> Hey ... I got something to show you.

> CORY
> *(defensively)*
> Like what?

> DES
> Check this.

DES pulls some cards out of his pocket: several birth certificates and medical cards.

> CORY
> What about 'em?

> DES
> This one says I'm ten. This one nine. It really messes the cops. They can't touch me.

CORY

For real?

DES

Wake up, man, they can't bust you till you're twelve. They can pick you up, but they gotta let you go. Like that's the law.

CORY
(impressed)
How'd you get 'em?

DES

I got 'em. There's a thing going tonight. You should come. You'll like.

CORY

Don't think so. *(bummed)* I gotta be somewhere.

DES

No fun for you.

DES hops on the bike. Kicks the starter. The bike won't turn over. Gives another kick. DES studies CORY's face for a trace of derision, but it's not there. DES laughs.

DES

Piece a crap.

DES takes the bike, gives it a shove and it topples into the water.

24. Interior. Examination Room. Video Image.

DES is restlessly moving in his seat.

THERAPIST *(off-screen)*:
How many days in a week, Des?

DES

Two.

THERAPIST *(off-screen)*:
Don't play me, Des.

DES
… Seven.

THERAPIST *(off-screen)*:
Great. Can you name them?

DES
Days of the week: Sunday, Monday, Thursday
... Friday, Saturday, Sunday. Happy?

THERAPIST *(off-screen)*:
Thanks. How many months in a year?

DES
Twelve.

THERAPIST *(off-screen)*:
Can you name them?

DES
I don't feel like it.

THERAPIST *(off-screen)*:
C'mon, give it a try.

DES
The twelve months?
(thinks; really trying)
April, June, May ... December ... July, March,
August, November ... *(thinks)* February.

THERAPIST *(off-screen)*:
Finished?

DES
Yeah. Those are the months.

25. Interior. Cory's House/Dining Room. Night.

CORY mopes over his salad at the table of this presentable, work-ing-class home. VINCE sits at the table. NONNY, three, VINCE's daughter, neatly picks at her meal. CORY's mother, JUDY, early thirties, holds the baby in one arm and pours NONNY some milk.

JUDY
Cory, eat something.

CORY
I hate rabbit food.

JUDY
It's good for you.

CORY
It's good for him. Why should we go on a diet
just because he does?

VINCE
C'mon Cory, we all have to eat it.

CORY
(contemptuous)
Oh yeah, right.

JUDY
Just finish your meal so we can go to the meeting. Vince, either hold the baby or start clearing up.

VINCE nods and takes the infant.

CORY
Why should I go, he's the drunk.

JUDY
Cory, cut it, that's old news.

VINCE
(relenting)
… Look, if he doesn't wanna go, he should just stay home.

JUDY
(firmly)
We go as a family.

VINCE
There's no point in forcing him.
(off her shrug)
Stay here if you want, Cory. What do you say?

CORY
I hate lettuce.

26. Exterior. The Docks. Night.

The glow of the fire in barrels spills on the restless boys.

MOUSE
What are we waiting for?

DES
Till I say so.

JAMAL
Check this.

JAMAL pulls out a porno magazine. The kids gather around him.

MOUSE
Whoa, I'm in luuuv.

JAMAL
Love sucks, man, just pop 'em and drop 'em.

DES
Oh, Jamal'd piss himself if he really had to do
something. He wouldn't know where to start.

JAMAL
Piss on you.

MOUSE
Des's done it, man.

DES
Straight leg, sixty-nine, the works. Went all
night with that Linda chick. She was hot.

NICK
(to TAK)
Did he really?

*TAK gives an authoritative nod to the affirmative. The others are
impressed.*

DES
But Jamal here just gets the pictures. 'Cause he
ain't got the hardware.

JAMAL
(under his breath)
Eat me.

DES
Say it again.

JAMAL
(defiant)
You heard me.

*It's a challenge. The kids eye DES, wondering what he'll do. But
the standoff is interrupted by a strange, foreboding whistle from
TAK, sending a chill over the group. TAK moves his head ever so
slightly to his left. Everyone freezes, staring in that direction.
DES's eyes narrow. There's someone in the shadows.*

DES relaxes.

> DES
>
> Hey Cory, Man. Just in time.

CORY steps into the street lamp's yellowy light. The rest of the kids eye him suspiciously. JAMAL looks down at DES, confronting him again.

> JAMAL
>
> Who said he could come?

> DES
>
> Who says he can't?

He nods for CORY to step over. JAMAL eyes CORY, who towers over him, then shrinks away.

> DES
>
> Like I said, you ain't got the hardware.

JAMAL burns. DES gives NICK a paper matchbook. NICK opens it.

> NICK
> *(reads)*
> Thirty-one Fraser Street.

27. Interior. Abandoned House/Main Floor. Night.

The back door is kicked open. DES stands in the threshold. Moon and street-lamp light spill through the windows as the kids run through the place.

> DES
>
> Hey! Mouse!

MOUSE goes to DES and hands him a water bottle.

> DES
>
> Thanks, just what I needed.

But instead of taking a drink, DES sprays the contents around the floor.

> JAMAL
>
> How much we gettin'?

> DES
>
> Enough. Nick.

> NICK
> *(hesitating)*
> You sure?

DES

Nick!

DES holds out his hand. NICK gives him a wooden match. DES nonchalantly lights it.

DES

Make a wish.

DES tosses it.

MOUSE

Holy crap.

The gasoline ignites.

MOUSE
(scared)

Let's get outta here.

DES, fascinated, keeps squeezing the plastic bottle, feeding the flames.

NICK

Des, let's move. Des!

The bottle ignites and DES drops it, burning his hand.

DES

Shit!

He looks around at the increasingly dangerous fire. The flames have engulfed the back entrance.

DES

Front door.

They scramble through the growing flames toward the front door. JAMAL rushes over and shoulders it. Nothing. He frantically hits it again and again. The kids are in full panic.

CORY

Get outta the way.

Then, with a huge kick, CORY smashes the door open. The kids bolt into the night air.

28. Exterior. Outside the House. Night.

A crowd watches fire trucks spray down the burning building. Behind them, JAMAL and the rest of the crew watch the show. DES and CORY arrive and are quickly surrounded by their cohorts.

> JAMAL
You get it?

DES, unintimidated, smiles. Shows them the crisp fifty-dollar bill.

> DES
There's more where that came from.

TAK whistles. They look to him. He makes a circular motion with his finger. The kids look. Cops are moving through the crowd. The younger kids nervously melt into the crowd, vanishing in a flash. DES turns to CORY.

> DES
Look at 'em. Babies.

> CORY
For sure.

> DES
> *(pulls out an object)*
Hey ... Got something for you.

> CORY
> *(checks out the pager, impressed)*
A pager?

> DES
Not hooked up yet. But it will be.

> CORY
This mean I'm in?

> DES
> *(for real)*
Good backup.

CORY checks it out. He likes it a lot. He checks a button.

> CORY
> *(to DES)*
Hey, what's this do?

But DES is a million miles away, staring at the blaze. Hypnotized. Lost.

29. Interior. Cory's House/Playroom. Day.

A toy moon vehicle zooms across the floor, screeches to a halt. A foot comes down, flattening it. CORY looks at DES.

CORY
What'd you do that for?

DES
Somebody's gotta do it.

CORY
Yeah. Beat the brat to it.

And he pulverizes a Mechano-type tower. Holding a baseball bat DES picks up a model spaceship. Tosses it in the air.

DES
Engage!

He whacks it with the bat, it crumples into the wall. They hear a baby wail.

VINCE crosses in with NONNY, his three-year-old daughter.

VINCE
Hey, boys, we're taking Bobby to the doctor now. Keep an eye on your sister, alright Cory?

CORY
She's not my sister.

JUDY, holding the baby, steps in.

JUDY
Let's not argue. Just pull your weight.

VINCE
It's no problem, we can bring her with us.

JUDY
No, he's big enough to take some responsibility. We're gonna be late. Bye.

She heads out. VINCE tries to share an intimacy with his stepson. DES watches VINCE, fascinated.

VINCE
(to CORY)
Look ... it's the baby's first booster shot ... your mom's kinda nervous about it.

CORY
(coldly)
So?

VINCE
So we appreciate you doing this.

CORY
… We?

VINCE
(not biting)
Feed your friend something if he wants it.

And he goes. CORY fumes.

30. Interior. Cory's House/Living Room. Day.

CORY's hand is stretched out on the glass, in a frozen wave goodbye. Through his fingers, the car pulls away outside.

CORY
They're outta here.

CORY, in the living room, turns to see DES, hands and mouth full of food.

CORY
Found some food, eh?

NONNY rushes up to CORY.

NONNY
Play with me. Play with me!

CORY
Get lost.

He pulls her worn stuffed-sock monkey from her.

NONNY
Gimmee. Gimmee my monkey.

CORY holds it above her head, out of reach.

CORY
Come and get it.

NONNY
Daddy!

CORY
Your dad's gone. You got me now.

NONNY
(starting to snuffle)
Gimmee!

DES
Let her have it.

DES grabs the ratty plush toy from CORY, who heads to the TV. DES kneels down to NONNY, sharing a confidence.

> DES
>
> If you lose your monkey in the jungle, you know what happens?

NONNY, wide eyed, shakes her head "No."

> DES
>
> It's sitting there all alone in the dark and unh!
> *(he bites it)*
> Tiger lunch. If you want no dead monkey, hang on to it.

She nods seriously at the advice. He gives the monkey to her. Then gives her some candy out of his pocket.

> CORY
>
> Des!

CORY's blasting aliens in a bloody video game. DES grabs the other joystick and the two fire away.

> NONNY
>
> Daddy! Daddy!

> CORY
>
> Daddy's gone. Shut up.

She's about to snuffle again. DES turns to her.

> DES
>
> Hey, I know something we can do.

> CORY
>
> Like what?

> DES
>
> Fun.

31. Exterior. Railroad Tracks. Day.

The two boys frame the tiny child in an ominous silhouette as they walk on the dock-side train rails. NONNY is licking an ice cream cone, stuffed monkey slung over her shoulder.

> CORY
>
> Everything went to shit when Vince moved in, the stupid goof.

DES
How long's he been around?

CORY
Ever since he knocked up my mom.

DES
Least you're not stuck in a foster home.

CORY
You?

DES
No way. Never get me in one of those stinkin' pissholes.

CORY
What's your dad like?

DES
He's like dead.

32. Interior. Examination Room. Video Image.

DES, face on the table, has a sideways glance at a picture: a puppy's at the dining room table; a big dog's at the door.

THERAPIST *(off-screen)*:
Tell me what's in this picture.

DES
... Big dog's coming for dinner.

THERAPIST *(off-screen)*:
Does the big dog live here?

DES
Sometimes.

THERAPIST *(off-screen)*:
And what's for dinner?

DES
(smiling enigmatically)
The little dog.

33. Exterior. Middle-class Neighbourhood. Day.

A foreboding sign: NONNY's ice cream cone is melting on a perfect, freshly trimmed lawn.

CORY *(off-screen):*
(nervously)
It's taking too long. Let's skip it.
DES *(off-screen):*
No man. Relax, it's cool.
CORY *(off-screen):*
Come on, let's just get outta here.

DES and CORY are huddled by the rear entrance of an upper middle-class home. DES is crouched by the door. He's pushing a little pair of legs through the dog door.

DES
She's in, man.

The boys quickly stand and peer through the glass. NONNY, confused, is standing in the kitchen.. The boys whisper to her.

DES
Come on, here, the lock.

NONNY just stands there.

CORY
Over here, stupid!

NONNY scans the strange surroundings and starts to cry.

CORY
(freaked)
Stop it, you little spaz, just open the door!

DES lays down and sticks his face in the dog door.

34. Interior. Kitchen. Day. Continuing.

NONNY sees DES's face appear in the dog door.

DES
Hey, Nonny, how's the monkey doin?

NONNY
… Okay.

DES
Want me to check it make sure it's okay?

NONNY
Uh huh.

                         DES
            Then you gotta let me in.
                        CORY
            Hurry up!
                       NONNY
            'Kay.
                         DES
            Put your hand on the doorknob.
She does.

                         DES
            See that twisty thing on top your hand?
                       NONNY
            Uh huh.
                         DES
            Give that a turn.

*She does. Click. The door swings open. The boys are framed in the
doorway.*

                         DES
            Good girl.

35. Interior. House/Living Room. Day.

*CORY is at the stereo cabinet, dumping the CDs into a pillowcase.
DES smashes a lamp with a five iron. NONNY wanders around with
her monkey.*

                        CORY
            That's all of 'em. Let's go.
                         DES
            Smile.

He's focusing a camcorder on CORY.

                        CORY
            Hey, turn that off.
                         DES
            Why not?
                        CORY
                  (covering his face)
            Seriously, man.

> DES
> *(handing it to him)*
> You shoot it then.

36. Interior. House/Bedroom. Day. Camcorder Video Image.

DES is bouncing on the bed, in and out of the shaky frame.

> CORY *(off-screen)*:
> What are you doing?

> DES
> Thinking.

> CORY *(off-screen)*:
> 'Bout what?

DES holds up a finger for CORY to wait. He moves to the nightstand, his back to us. Opens the drawer and reaches in.

Suddenly DES whirls, a gun pointed at the camera. The video image careens wildly as the camera bounces on the floor.

Back to film.

> CORY
> You're nuts, man.

> DES
> Hey, pick it up, that's worth somethin'.

> CORY
> Screw you asshole.

> DES
> *(laughing)*
> Did I scare ya?

DES puts the gun and ammo in a pillowcase. Holds it out to CORY, who dumps in the camera.

> DES
> Check out time.

37. Exterior. House/Back Lane. Day.

DES and CORY hold their pillowcases as they head through the gate with NONNY.

> DES
> Good haul.

CORY
Are we clear?

DES
You know it.

CORY
Let's boot.

NONNY
My monkey.

CORY
We're going now.

NONNY
I need my monkey.

She starts to go back. CORY grabs her.

CORY
Listen, we gotta go.

NONNY
(crying)
I want my monkey.

CORY
Shut up, we gotta roll.

NONNY
Tiger's gonna eat it.

CORY
(shaking her)
I said shut your face!

NONNY
Monkey!

DES
(stopping him)
Let's just get it.

DES hides his case with the gun and camera under a bush. CORY walks back into the yard with his pillowcase, carelessly leaving it on the picnic table as they head back inside.

38. Interior. The House/Hallway. Day.

DES
You had it in the living room right?

NONNY

I dunno.

CORY

Did you leave it in the bathroom?

NONNY

I dunno.

She spots the monkey under a chair.

NONNY

There it is!

DES

Okay, we got it, let's roll!

He grabs the monkey, turns to go ... and looks straight at two cops.
Busted.

39. Interior. Police Station/Youth Division. Day.

A child's hand is pushed against a sheet of white paper. An adult
hand pulls it up by the wrist, leaving a palm print in black ink. The
other hand is pressed down. Two large adult hands pick up the pair
of palm prints, two little hands in a sea of white. The hands belong
to CONSTABLE KOSTASH, thirty, who takes the document and
places it in a folder.

The Youth Division office is an airless room filled with old sloppy
desks and walls covered with mug shots of kids. One set of photos
covers known gang members, another set is car thieves. Another of
repeat B&Es. CORY is terror-struck as KOSTASH roughly pulls
his wrists, handcuffing him and DES in turn.

DES

Let us go, we didn't do nuthin'!

KOSTASH

What were you doing in that house then?

DES

We were gettin his sister's toy monkey. You
saw it!

KOSTASH

And how'd the monkey get in there?

DES

She dropped it.

KOSTASH snorts derisively.

CHOU *(off-screen)*:
Well will you look who's here. Smile!

A flash goes off. Police CONSTABLE CHOU, mid-twenties, rips the Polaroid print of the boys out of the camera.

CHOU:
Welcome to the Wall of Shame, you little knobs.

CHOU sticks the photo up on the wall with the other B&Es as CLARKE, the school liaison officer strides in.

KOSTASH
Keep movin' you bozos.

CORY
(scared)
Where you takin' us?

DES
Nowhere, they can't keep us here.

KOSTASH
That's right, smartass.

CLARKE
(to CORY)
What are you doing here anyway, hangin' with this loser?

CORY
(fearfully)
What happened to my sister?

KOSTASH
Hear that? He cares about his sister! Whoa!

CLARKE
She's with a social worker upstairs. Man, you really blew this one.

DES
Let us go. You can't keep us here!

KOSTASH
(poking him)
Not yet, Desi Boy, but when the clock strikes twelve, you're mine.

DES gives him the finger.

CLARKE
Believe me, pal, if you don't slow down, you'll
be dead before you're twenty.

DES
Promise?

*CLARKE, disgusted, shakes his head and joins KOSTASH by the
coffee machine. DES doesn't take his eyes off him as CHOU comes
to the boys. He shoves them down. The rough treatment is getting
to CORY.*

DES keeps eyeing KOSTASH and CLARKE.

KOSTASH
Why do you waste your time with that little
shitrat?

CLARKE
(shaking his head)
You ever seen where he comes from? It's like
friggin' Beirut.

KOSTASH
Cry me a river, man. Lots of us scrambled
outta way worse holes than that little scumbag.

CLARKE
Your scumbag's eleven.

*KOSTASH derisively slurps his coffee. They've had this argument
before.*

KOSTASH
Save it, man. All I wanna do is lock the mutant
up.

As CHOU pushes them out, DES watches KOSTASH and CLARKE.

CLARKE
Great, bust 'em in kindergarten, might as well
be waitin' with a warrant in the delivery room.

KOSTASH
(grinning)
Can you do that?

40. Interior. Interrogation Room. Day.

Claustrophobic gray with black marks on walls and ceiling. The boys are handcuffed back to back in the room's two beat-up metal chairs. CORY's trembling.

                    DES
        C'mon, breathe or something, man.

                    CORY
                    (ashen)
        What're they gonna do to us?

                    DES
        Nothing. They got no choice but let us go.

                    CORY
        Then what are we still doin' here?

                    DES
        They're just lettin' us stew.

                    CORY
        Why'd you go back, we were home free!

                    DES
                    (realizing)
        ... You never been here before.

                    CORY
        Yeah! What about it?

                    DES
        My first time here, I pissed my pants.

                    CORY
        Bullshit ... really?

                    DES
        You could see the puddle and everything.

                    CORY
        Gross.

                    DES
        Yeah, I was like six.

                    CORY
        No way!

CORY's regained a little of his confidence. CHOU and KOSTASH come in.

CHOU:
We found the pillowcase of CDs. All we wanna
know is what you did with the rest of the stuff.

DES
We didn't take nuthin'.

CHOU:
Oh, you didn't take nuthin', huh! Well, we'll
find out soon enough. You see, the owners left
an itemized list of everything.

DES
Yeah, right, they haven't been there in a month.

CHOU, astonished, looks at KOSTASH.

KOSTASH
(to CHOU)
I told you, the kid's a knob. Been casing the
joint.

DES
I'm underage, I got ID.

CORY
You can't touch us, right?

KOSTASH
That's right, we can't do anything to you. Ex-
cept for this.

*KOSTASH nods. CHOU reaches behind the door and brings out a
phone. Hands it to KOSTASH.*

KOSTASH
Let's call your mommy, Cory.

*CORY turns pale. Frozen. KOSTASH punches numbers into the
phone.*

KOSTASH
One ringadingy. Two ringadingy …

*CORY starts to cry. KOSTASH, satisfied, looks at CHOU. His
tactic is having the desired effect.*

DES
When's it my turn to call?

KOSTASH
Shut up! We'll deal with you later, big boy.

DES slumps back in his chair, furious and frustrated.

KOSTASH
… Four ringa—Bingo.
(to phone)
Hello, Mrs. Welch? Police Constable Kostash,
Youth Division. Your son wants to have a word
with you.

Hands the receiver to CORY.

CORY
(on the phone)
… Mom? … the Police Station … yeah, yeah,
I'm okay, she is too … Mom, don't cry, c'mon
don't worry … Please, Mom, please, don't,
don't—

*The line goes dead. He looks at the receiver. KOSTASH, contented,
hangs it up. The cops leave. CORY watches the door close.*

CORY
(upset)
Oh man, she's gonna kill me.

He hears a soft breathing. Strains to look at DES.

CORY
Des … Des?

DES has drifted off to sleep.

Fade to black.

In darkness:

VINCE *(V.O.)*
I can't believe this.

As DES blurrily opens his eyes, reveal …

41. Interior. The Interrogation Room. Day.

DES watches a grim-faced VINCE stand over CORY.

VINCE
What was in your head, taking Nonny.

CORY
You always say not to leave her alone.

VINCE
Cory, you coulda been risking her life.

CORY
That's all you care about. *(mutters)* Pig.

DES watches VINCE carefully, waiting to see what he'll do. But VINCE just breathes, exhales in a sigh. DES is astonished.

VINCE
Okay, let's get outta here. Officer?

CHOU steps in, uncuffs CORY. DES laughs.

DES
See, they can't touch us!

CORY, realizing that DES is right, grins at his pal. VINCE, catching this interaction, burns, but heads out the door.

DES
See you tomorrow, Bud!

This ignites VINCE who whirls around. Inflamed, he eyeballs DES.

VINCE
(furious)
Stay away from him, you hear me? I don't
want to see you near him ever again.

DES just stares at him.

THERAPIST *(V.O.)*
Do you remember your dad?

DES *(V.O.)*
No.

THERAPIST (V.O.)
What do you know about him?

42. Interior. Examination Room. Video Image. Continuing.

DES's feet dig into the carpet.

THERAPIST:
... What do you know about him, Des?

DES
Burned up in a fire.

THERAPIST *(off-screen)*:
What was he doing?

> DES
> Putting it out.

> THERAPIST *(off-screen)*:
> He was a fireman? *(off DES's nod)* Sounds like
> a hero ... Des?

> DES
> I dunno.

43. Interior. Police Car. Day. Travelling.

KOSTASH is driving, CHOU shotgun. DES is in the back, kicking the seat. CHOU can feel it.

> DES
> Hey you buggers, let me off here, this is my
> stop.

> CHOU:
> Just sit still and shut up.

> DES
> Who's gonna make me, bug head. Bug sucker.

> KOSTASH
> I gotta get me one of those muzzles from Dog
> Squad.

> DES
> Hey, Kostash, I hear you give great blowjobs.
> You wanna blow me now? Blow me!

> KOSTASH
> *(to CHOU)*
> Just keep imagining him nice and quiet on a
> slab.

> DES
> I hear all the faggots love you two. I hear you
> love gettin' the pants down and suck suck
> sucking.

CHOU turns around, glaring at DES.

> CHOU:
> Say what you want, punk, we're taking you
> home to momma.

DES spits in his face. CHOU reaches over the seat and collars him.

CHOU:
You little—

KOSTASH
(holding him back)
Relax. He's playin' you.

CHOU, steaming, wipes off his face. DES eyes him.

DES
I want a lawyer.

44. Interior. Des's House. Day.

The cops move with DES through the hallway. They hear the sound of gunshots.

DOLLY is intently playing a video game, blasting her opponents.

CHOU:
Excuse me, ma'am.

She keeps playing.

KOSTASH
(loudly)
Hello there.

DOLLY has a glance at them, goes back to her game.

CHOU:
Are you Mrs. Bowen?

DOLLY
No.

CHOU:
Are you his mother?

DOLLY
No.

KOSTASH
Any relation to this boy?

DOLLY
Grandmother.

The cops look at each other, bewildered. The woman's got to be in her early forties.

CHOU:
We'd like to talk to his mother.

> DOLLY
>
> You can't.

> KOSTASH
>
> Why's that?

> DOLLY
>
> She's out.

> KOSTASH
>
> Look, we just picked this kid up in the middle
> of a burglary.

DOLLY wastes a gunman.

> KOSTASH
>
> Hello?

She pulverizes another one.

> CHOU:
>
> Ma'am?

Bangbangbang. She snuffs five guerrillas. KOSTASH turns to CHOU, who is in a small state of shock.

> KOSTASH
>
> This is the house. This the grandmother. Dead
> end.

The cops go out the door. DES kicks it closed behind them.

He turns back to DOLLY who's still playing the video game.

> DES
>
> My turn.

> DOLLY
>
> I'm playing.

> DES
>
> My game.

> DOLLY
>
> So?

DES burns.

45. Exterior. The Docks. Day. Video Image.

Rats sniff at a rotting fish on the weathered wood. Crack of a gunshot. The rats scatter as one of their brethren is splattered by a perfect shot.

DES proudly checks the hand gun.

DES
Didja get it?

TAK nods "Yes."

MOUSE
Wicked shot, Des!

He pats DES on the back. DES shoves him away.

DES
Gimmee some space.

MOUSE
(instantly recovering)
There's another one, get it!

SAM
No, over there, get that one!

DES glowers at them. Back to film. TAK's been taping on DES's stolen camcorder.

JAMAL
If you're not gonna do it, let me.

DES
What?

NICK
It's his turn.

DES
I'm playing.

JAMAL
I been waiting an hour.

DES
My gun.

JAMAL
Know why he's bein' such a dink?

NICK
Why?

JAMAL
His boyfriend isn't comin' anymore.

DES whirls, pointing the gun at JAMAL.

MOUSE
(nervously)
I saw him, Des, he was walking with his dad.

DES
Not his dad. Just the guy dicking his mom.

DES laughs, turns and fires at a rat. Bangbangbang.

46. Interior. Cory's House/Living room. Day.

Lupo the butcher, on the TV screen, slices off his thumb and spurts blood.

CORY, listlessly watching, hears voices from another room.

JUDY *(off-screen)*:
My kid's running wild with a drug-dealing thug
and you're gonna be reasonable.

The phone starts to ring. CORY gets up, going to answer it.

Ring. The bedroom door opens and VINCE emerges, continuing the argument.

VINCE
What do you wanna do, ground the kid for the
rest of his life?

Ring. JUDY appears in the doorway.

JUDY
He doesn't need a friend, he needs a father.

CORY reaches for the phone but VINCE snaps it up first, his repressed anger surfacing.

VINCE
I told you to leave Cory alone!

CORY
Lemmee talk to him.

VINCE slams down the phone.

47. Exterior. A Phone Booth. Day.

DES smashes the handset against the phone box.

DES
Stupid bastard!

He smashes it again and again.

48. Interior. Cory's Bedroom. Day.

CORY, bummed out, slams the door, punches on some music. Knock on the bedroom door.

VINCE

Cory—Cory!

CORY turns up the volume.

49. Interior. Examination Room. Video Image.

DES sits in front of four boxes.

Each box has a line drawing of a figure on it and a name label: "My Mom," "My Grandma," "Cory," and the last box has the figure crossed out.

THERAPIST (off-screen):

Mom, Grandma, Cory, and this box we'll call Nobody. So now I'll give you a card and you put it in the first person you think of, okay? ... Cheerful.

We see his hand take a card with "Cheerful" written on it. He puts it in the slot at the top of "My Grandma."

THERAPIST (off-screen):

Takes care of me.

DES puts the card in "Mother."

THERAPIST (off-screen):

Understands me.

He puts it in "Cory."

THERAPIST (off-screen):

Is never there.

Puts it in "Nobody."

THERAPIST (off-screen):

Loves me.

DES puts it in "Mother."

THERAPIST (off-screen):

I'd like to kill.

Puts it in "Nobody."

THERAPIST (off-screen):

I'm happy when this person is around.

Pause. Puts it in "Cory."

50. Interior. Cory's Bedroom. Dusk.

Bored, CORY flips through a comic book. He hears a quiet buzzing sound. He strains to hear it. Searches in a pile of dirty clothes. Finally he feels something in the pocket of some torn up jeans. The pager. He smiles.

51. Exterior/Interior. Cory's House/The Truck. Dusk.

The window opens. CORY crawls out. He looks around, curiously searching for DES. Carefully pads toward the street, where VINCE's carpet cleaning truck is parked. The truck starts, DES appears behind the wheel.

> DES
> Let's go for a ride.

CORY smiles, then jumps in. They slap hands. DES hands CORY a lit joint and punches on the radio. They slap hands. DES floors it and the truck squeals away.

52. Interior/Exterior. Truck/City Streets. Series of Shots.

The music from the radio drives the images through their joy-ride through the warehouse section of town.

53. Interior/Exterior. The Truck/Warehouse District. Dusk. Travelling.

DES guns the truck through the warehouse section. He hoots as they pass some hookers.

> DES
> Hey, Baby, how much for a blow?

To their delight, she gives him the finger. Chortling, DES screeches around a corner.

> CORY
> Hey watch it, man!

> DES
> … You got some smokes?

Brendan Fletcher as Des (left) and Myles Ferguson as Cory.

Top: Des (left) threatens the Dink held by Sam (middle) and
Mouse. Bottom: Des and Cory go for a spin.

Top: Des (left) shares a covert smoke with Tak.
Bottom: Cory in the custody of Constable Chou.

Top: Des (left) and Cory watch the fire. Bottom: Director
Stephen Surjik discuss a scene with Brendan Fletcher.

CORY

No.

DES

I need 'em.

CORY

Well I don't got 'em.

DES

Then I gotta get 'em.

DES heads straight for a building. CORY's eyes open wide.

CORY

Hey slow down, man!

DES laughs.

CORY

What're you doin?

DES howls. CORY tries to put on his seat belt as the truck pops up the curb, over the sidewalk and crashes through the glass of a small grocery store. The old alarm bell rings.

DES

Shit!

CORY

Cool!

DES

Guard the truck.

CORY watches DES jump out and run into the store. In a flash, DES emerges from the store holding two cartons of cigarettes.

54. Interior. Des's House/Living Room. Night.

RUTH is spreading wet laundry around to dry. She looks up as DES enters.

RUTH

Hey, you know what time it is?

DES

No.

RUTH

Me neither.

DES
I got something for you.

He puts a carton of cigarettes down on the table.

RUTH
Aw, Des, that's sweet a you. *(hugs him)* Getcher self something to eat.

DES
Already ate.

55. Exterior/Interior. Des's House/Truck. Night.

DES exits the house, carrying the pillowcase from the house job. The truck looks empty. DES opens the door. CORY is nervously eating a candy bar, slumped down below the dashboard, keeping out of sight. Seeing DES, he instantly sits back up.

DES
Know what we gotta do? Get 'tooed!

CORY
Got to! Money?

DES
Covered.

56. Exterior/Interior. Chet's House/Front Door. Night.

Heavy metal is blasting from the party inside the druggie house. CORY and DES stand on the porch as a very stoned CHET pulls the camcorder out of the pillowcase.

CHET
Yeah, this is uh … I seen better at the dump.

CHET sticks the lens in DES's face. DES pretends to like it.

CORY
You ain't seen shit.

CHET lifts an eyebrow, chuckles.

CHET
Oo, big man! Alright, fifty.

Reaches in his pocket, pulls out some bills.

DES
(pissed)
Screw you then.

CHET
Hey hey, no need to get nasty. Didn't know
you were so desperate. *(beat)* Seventy.

CHET pulls out another twenty, smiling.

CHET
A pleasure doin' business with you boys.

CHET drops the money on the ground and closes the door.

DES
Turd sucker.

They move down the porch steps. DES starts for the truck but CORY motions him to the window. DES looks at him quizzically.

CORY
Hey Des!

57. Interior/Exterior. Chet's House. Night.

The boys watch CHET toss the camcorder down. A very stoned teenage girl kisses him and draws him out of the room. Outside, CORY turns to DES.

CORY
Payback.

They grin and tap fists. CORY carefully opens the window.

DES
You're bad, man.

CORY grins and climbs in. Inside, CORY carefully pads across the room. Grabs the camcorder. DES helps him through the window.

DES
Come on!

CORY scrambles to get out. His jacket's caught on the sill. CHET appears behind him in the doorway. CORY leaps out, leaving a torn shred of his jacket.

58. Interior. Makeshift Tattoo Parlor. Day.

A burning skull is tattooed into an arm with the logo, "Born to Die." DES is watching critically as FAKIR, the quasi tattoo artist, puts the final touches on CORY. DES checks his identical tattoo with CORY's.

                    CORY
          How's it look?

                    DES
          Total value.

DES takes the twice-stolen camcorder out of a sack.

                    DES
          It's all yours.

                    FAKIR
                (checking it)
          Remember to keep those clean and use skin
          cream.

                    DES
                (laughing)
          Good tip.

He joins CORY at the mirror. It reflects DES and CORY admiring their shoulders together.

59. Interior/Exterior. Truck/Cory's House. Night.

DES cuts the engine. The music dies.

The headlights black out as the truck silently rolls around the corner and pulls to a stop in front of CORY's house.

                    DES
          Nuthin' stops us.

                    CORY
          Nuthin'.

They slap hands. CORY looks ahead.

                    DES
          Shit.

DES tries to put the truck in drive but VINCE has the door open and yanks DES out, throwing him against the hood. The dam has burst.

                    VINCE
          I told you to stay away from him!

                    DES
          Lemmee go!

                    VINCE
You're killing any chance that kid has! You
know what you're doin' to this family!

                    DES
Back off!

VINCE stares, horrified. DES is aiming the gun at him.

                    VINCE
                  (carefully)
You shouldn't be waving that around. *(slowly)*
What do you want?

DES doesn't budge. CORY watches, frozen.

                    VINCE
Come on, put it away.

                    DES
                   (hyper)
I'll put it away, I'll put it in you!

                    VINCE
                (backing away)
Cool it, alright, just cool it. Cory, talk to him.

                    DES
Nobody dicks with me!

                    VINCE
                  (whispers)
Don't ... don't ... please ...

DES points the gun. Right at VINCE's throat.

                    DES
Bang.

*VINCE stares in shock. DES peacocks away, feeling like God.
CORY looks at VINCE. Then follows DES.*

60. Exterior. Cory's House. Day.

*The trashing Vince's truck took last night looks harsher in the
morning light. An investigating OFFICER inspects it. CLARKE
talks to VINCE and JUDY.*

                    JUDY
He's been out all night. We haven't heard a
thing from him.

> CLARKE
> Don't worry, he'll show up.

> VINCE
> *(determined)*
> That boy's leash just got very short.

JUDY and VINCE look at each other. Then JUDY turns to CLARKE.

> JUDY
> Find my son.

61. Exterior. East-end Street. Day.

The DINK from the schoolyard is trapped by the boys.

> CORY
> That's it? You're tellin' me that's all you got?

> DINK
> Uh huh.

> CORY
> He's lying, Des. He's lying to me.

> DES
> I hate liars. Gimmee it.

> CORY
> You serious?

> DES
> Gimmee the gun.

> DINK
> No, please.

CORY hands DES a dangerous looking weapon.

> DES
> You lie, you die.

DES puts the muzzle a couple of inches away from the DINK's face.

> DINK
> No.

> DES
> Kiss it goodbye, punk.

And DES pulls the trigger, spraying the DINK with water. DES and CORY crack up. The DINK stares, shocked.

DES
Ten bucks tomorrow. Or you drown for real.

CORY lets him go. The DINK runs off. They're still laughing.

DES
You see that, he pissed himself.

CORY
(grabbing the gun)
No you pissed yourself.

Water squirts out, showering DES.

DES
Dinkhole!

Laughing, DES wrestles CORY for the gun. But a car honking stops their play. CHET's pulled up in his Comet.

CHET
Hey you bozos, c'mere.

CORY, freaked, glimpses at DES. DES rolls his eyes. No sweat. He heads over to CHET, CORY following his lead.

DES
Hey, Chet man, just in time. Got a couple drops
of window pane on ya?

CHET
Maybe later. Alright, listen. Some gluehead
whipped into my place and lifted that camera
you guys sold me.

DES
That sucks bigtime.

CHET
Not bigger than the price'll be paid for the
deed. Check this.

CHET shows them the ripped piece of Cory's jacket.

CORY
What is it?

CHET
This is a piece of the perpetrator. Either of you
seen it before?

          CORY
         (quietly)
No.

          CHET
Huh?

          CORY
No!

          DES
Hey! Chet, man, I'll find out who the goof is.
And give him to you. It'll be like a birthday
present.

          CHET
Yeah? Well, not for the perp.

CHET squeals off. CORY, grey, looks at DES.

          DES
Guy's a pure chump, man.

62. Exterior. Street Near Des's House. Day.

*DES and CORY walk down the street. CORY is shooting water high
in the air with his squirt gun.*

          CORY
Bam! Seagal kicks ass.

          DES
Seagal's wank shit. Van Damme.

          CORY
Seagal knows guns.

          DES
He knows dick, man. Van Damme's real. In
Hard Target—that guy with the missile
launcher? Van Damme took him out for real.
Guy was bagged and tagged.
     (does a high kick)
Death kick to the throat!

          CORY
Van Damme couldn't take Seagal.

DES

In two seconds. Seagal's fake. He's a fag. *Under Siege* my ass.

DES freezes. CORY looks. Doesn't get it.

CORY

What is it?

DES

Check the car beside my house.

CORY

Yeah, so?

DES stealthily moves to the sedan. Its styling is pretty sleek and the paint job brighter than the average unmarked car. DES points at the computer unit beside the driver's seat.

DES

Vince ratted.

CORY

Sorry, man.

DES moves to the side of the house.

CORY

What you want me to do?

CORY's still holding the squirt gun.

DES

Nuthin'. Just go.

DES pulls up a rotting board. There's a hole beneath. And a plastic bag. DES reaches to the small of his back, revealing the revolver. For an instant CORY compares his squirt gun to the real thing.

DES puts the revolver in the plastic bag. Covers it with the board. DES goes to the basement window.

DES

Later.

And he crawls in the window.

63. Interior. Des's House/Basement. Day.

DES crawls into the basement from the window, and furtively moves across the floor, past one of his tiger drawings, sketched on the roughed-in wall. As he moves, we hear DES and the therapist speak during a therapy session.

> DES *(V.O.)*
> It never sleeps. One eye always open. Anything comes near me or my mom, it rips them to shit.

> THERAPIST *(V.O.)*
> So you can sleep without anybody coming in?

> DES *(V.O.)*
> Kills them.

> THERAPIST *(V.O.)*
> Who might come in?

> DES *(V.O.)*
> Nobody.

> THERAPIST *(V.O.)*
> Who's Nobody?

> DES *(V.O.)*
> Nobody.

With incredible stealth, DES moves up the steps. And peeks through the door at the top of the stairway.

64. Interior. Des's House/Hallway. Day.

A POLICE CONSTABLE is going through a box near the basement door, which opens just a crack. DES peeks out.

> CLARKE *(off-screen)*:
> Look, the boy stole a truck and pulled a gun ...

> RUTH *(off-screen)*:
> Everybody's a monster to you cops. You see a psycho. I see my kid!

The cop moves away and DES gets a clear look at what's going on.

RUTH is in the kitchen with CONSTABLE CLARKE, and a social worker, BOURGET.

> RUTH
> *(continuing)*
> So who says he pulled a gun? You got witnesses?

CLARKE
Aw look, the kid's a holy terror and it's just
getting worse.

RUTH
What do you want me to do—tie him up and
drag him to work with me?

CLARKE
(losing patience)
If you can't handle the kid, give him up.

RUTH
I'm his mother.

CLARKE
Then act like it.

BOURGET:
Put him in care. It's his only chance.

RUTH
I know about care. I've been there. You wanna
know about those stinking pissholes? About
foster parents? About foster daddies? Where
the hell you think Des came from?

*They're both struck dumb by the revelation. DES is completely
confused by what she just said. Clearly this is news to him too.
Something's been wrenched deep inside him.*

BOURGET *(off-screen)*:
(shaken)
We're just trying to do what's best for your
son.

RUTH *(off-screen)*:
Get the hell outta my house. Get out!

*Pale with shock and worry, he watches the authorities hurriedly
exit.*

65. Exterior. Des's House. Day.

As the disturbed CLARKE and BOURGET leave.

66. Interior. Des's House/Kitchen. Day.

A kitchen knife smacks into a slab of frozen hamburger. RUTH is at the counter, throwing back some straight vodka, and with each whack she gets angrier. DES moves into the doorway, still a bit flipped from what she said.

> DES
> *(quietly)*
> Mom ... Mommy what were you saying to them?

RUTH smacks the meat again.

> RUTH
> About what?

> DES
> 'Bout the foster home. 'Bout my dad.

She looks at him, still holding the knife.

> RUTH
> I said he was a piece of shit just like you. Only difference is he's a dead piece of shit! What the hell you think I am, bringing the cops down on me?

> DES
> I didn't know they were comin'.

> RUTH
> You got no brains gettin' caught like that— wavin' guns!

She throws the meat across the floor.

> DES
> I didn't do nuthin', Mom, I swear it.

> RUTH
> You make 'em think I'm unfit.

DES goes closer to her, wanting her to hold him.

> DES
> *(every bit the child)*
> No I don't, Mom, you're fit, you are, Mom.

> RUTH
> I'm trash, trash, trash. That's what I am!

DES
No, Mom—

RUTH
Trash, just like you!

She swings the knife wildly, the blade slashing DES across the chest. DES, in shock, watches the blood flow. RUTH, sobbing, drops the knife, embracing DES.

RUTH
Oh Baby I'm sorry. I'm sorry, I'm sorry, I'm sorry ...

Fade to black.

67. Interior. Hospital Recovery Room. Night.

DES lies in a bed, just stitched up. A NURSE, in her twenties, gently checks DES's dressing. The bandages cover a big part of his chest.

NURSE
You just took a lot of stitches.

DES
Yeah.

NURSE
What happened?

DES
I got jumped.

NURSE
Tough out there, huh? Did you see who did it?

DES
Three guys. They took my wallet.

NURSE
Well, you should try and get some sleep.

As the nurse exits, CLARKE and BOURGET move into the room.

CLARKE
Des?

BOURGET:
Hey, Des.

DES
Where's Cory?

CLARKE
Back at home.

DES
I wanna see him.

CLARKE
That won't be happening for long time.

DES
I didn't do nuthin'.

CLARKE
I know.

BOURGET:
You're going to a place called the Children's
House. You've been put in Care, Des.

DES
You can't. You gotta have parents' permission.

CLARKE
We've got it, Des.

DES
No way you'd get it. From who?

CLARKE
From your mother, pal.

DES
You're lying.

BOURGET:
It's true.

DES
No way. She wouldn't.

CLARKE
She just signed the forms.

*CLARKE pulls the papers out of a file. DES gapes, not believing
what he's seeing. He rips them up.*

DES
No. No way.

68. Interior. Children's House/Rita's Office. Video Image.

DES is staring at the floor.

THERAPIST *(off-screen)*:
Hello, Des.

DES rocks in his chair, ignoring her.

THERAPIST *(off-screen)*:
Hello, Des. Des?

DES
Hello. Fuck you.

The video image shifts to film. And we're now in real time. And for the first time we see RITA KAPELI, the therapist, a determined thirty-five-year-old.

RITA
(without flinching)
I'd like to show you some cards, Des.

DES grabs a pencil off her desk.

RITA
(calmly)
All you have to do is tell me what they make you think of.

He stabs it into the chair.

RITA
I can turn the camera off if it's bothering you, Des.

She turns and indicates the video camera mounted on a tripod. He snaps the pencil in two.

RITA
Or I can leave it on.

He throws the eraser end of it.

RITA
(not missing a beat)
It doesn't matter what you do, Des, I still get paid for being here.

DES just looks at her.

RITA
That's all for today. See you next time.

She moves to the door. He pockets the sharp end of the pencil. She opens the door for him. Waits for him to go.

69. Interior. Children's House/Dining Room. Day.

Dinner has been served at the table where DES sits with four other kids, aged five to eleven. LAURA, late twenties, a rather wry child-care worker, is there with them. The other kids are digging in. DES just sits there, his plate empty, rubbing the now infected tattoo.

> LAURA:
> Why don't you have something to eat, Des?

DES shrugs. She hands him the bowl of french fries.

> LAURA:
> The fries are good tonight. Have some.

DES starts spooning fries on his plate. He keeps doing it, methodically, until his plate is overflowing with them.

> LAURA:
> That's alright, Des, you can have as much as
> you want. How about some chicken?

LAURA offers DES the platter. DES stares at it: he can't figure it out. What's the angle? DES just looks at the plate. LAURA notices his arm.

> LAURA:
> What happened to your arm, Des?

> DES
> Nuthin'.

> LAURA:
> You should let the nurse have a look at that.

70. Interior. Children's House/Des's Room. Night.

DES paces like a caged animal in the room. He sniffs at the clean little-boy pyjamas he's wearing. Feels the starched white sheets. Ponders the poster of a lioness nuzzling her cub. There's a knock on the door. DES stiffens and whirls, ready for anything.

> DES
> What?

LAURA sticks her head in the door.

> LAURA:
> Just wanted to say goodnight before lights out.

DES
So?

LAURA:
Sleep tight.

LAURA closes the door. He listens to be sure she's gone. Then he goes to his bed, and furiously rips the bed apart, grabs a blanket and goes into the closet, shutting the door behind him.

71. Interior. Children's House/Rita's Office. Day.

DES is looking at the card with the big dog coming to dine with the little dog.

RITA
And who's coming to dinner?

DES
... the big dog.

RITA
And what's for dinner?

DES
The little dog.

RITA
Okay. Let's look at another one.

She hands him another test picture: three monkeys in a tug of war. Two on one side, one bigger monkey on the other.

DES
Tug of war. Two against one.

RITA
Who's going to win?

DES
Two.

RITA
What will the loser do?

DES
Kill 'em.

RITA
They're just playing.

DES
So?

RITA
(breathes)
… Very good. Want to look at another one?

DES
No.

RITA
You were doing really well at it.

DES
Boring.

RITA
Is it boring?

DES
Boring shit.

RITA
Okay. Let's try something different.

DES
Bite me.

RITA
Fine. We'll continue next time.

She waits for DES to go. He's a little confused. Didn't expect to be kicked out.

RITA
(firmly)
I'll see you tomorrow, Des.

DES, a little disappointed, leaves. As soon as he's gone, RITA ejects the cassette and adds it to the small pile on DES's shelf.

72. Interior. Children's House/Games Room. Day.

DES stands across from MITCH, thirty, another child-care worker, at the ping pong table. Behind them, kids are playing Foosball, cards, board games.

MITCH
Ready?

DES
Yeah.

MITCH serves it. The ball sails by DES.

> MITCH
> That's okay, I've got another one.

MITCH serves it again. The ball skids past DES who goes to it. Then he stomps on the ball, flattening it.

> MITCH
> Hey, Des, what's going on?

> DES
> Nuthin'.

> MITCH
> You know the rules, Des. You want to learn to play, we'll teach you. You want to wreck the stuff, you're outta here.

DES starts to go.

> MITCH
> See you tomorrow.

73. Interior. Children's House/Dining Room. Day.

DES sullenly eats his food, ignoring the chatter of the kids around him.

From the doorway, RITA watches DES. She turns and goes.

74. Interior. Children's House/Washroom. Night.

DES stares at the washroom mirror, new toothbrush in hand. He unwraps the toothbrush and picks up the toothpaste tube. Bypassing the brush, he puts the tube to the mirror, smearing paste across the glass.

75. Interior. Children's House/Nursing Room. Day.

The nurse speaks very gently to DES.

> NURSE
> We just need to take that bandage off and make sure everything is healing nicely.

DES eyes her suspiciously.

> NURSE
> I can't do it unless you take your shirt off, Des.

DES doesn't move.

> NURSE
> What happened to your arm there, Des?

> DES
> Nuthin'.

> NURSE
> Looks like you've got an infection. That must really hurt. Can I have a look?

Pause. DES allows her to examine his shoulder.

> DES
> ... Is it wrecked now?

> NURSE
> I don't know, we'll have to wait and see how it heals. Will you let me clean it up?

DES shrugs.

> DES
> It's prob'ly wrecked.

And he lets her start cleaning the wound.

76. Interior. Children's House/Lounge. Day.

DES observes RITA, on a break, finishing up a game of solitaire. He moves closer, fascinated as she struggles to shuffle the deck.

> RITA
> Oh! Would you believe my brother was a card shark? I guess it's just not in my genes.

DES nods, expressionless. She hands him the deck. He taps it on the table and expertly shuffles it. A total pro.

> RITA
> How did you learn to do that?

> DES
> Just did.

> RITA
> Could you teach me?

DES is momentarily disarmed.

> DES
> ... Okay.

He hands her back the deck.

RITA

Okay. Now what do I do?

DES

You bend 'em. Like this.

Guiding her hands.

DES

Okay, let go.

She does. Surprise. It works.

RITA

Let's do it again.

Once again, he covers her hands with his, guiding her.

RITA

Wait'll my brother sees this!

DES can barely conceal the sense of pride and satisfaction.

77. Interior. Children's House/Rita's Office. Day.

DES is in front of the camera, making faces. RITA enters, catching him in the act.

RITA

You seem a little excited today.

DES

No, not really.

RITA comes to her place, noticing a pack of cigarettes on her desk.

RITA

Hey! What's this?

DES

(sitting down)

For you.

RITA

A present?

DES

Uh huh.

RITA

How did you know I smoked?

> DES
>
> Could tell.
>
> RITA
>
> Well, thank you very much, Des.
>   *(beat)*
> Where did you get them?
>
> DES
>
> Got them.
>
> RITA
>
> Did you have to leave the grounds?
>
> DES
>
> No.
>
> RITA
>
> Did you take them from someone?
>
> DES
>
> No.
>
> RITA
>
> Do you like to give presents?
>
> DES
>
> Yeah. Sometimes.
>
> RITA
>
> To who?
>
> DES
>
> Whoever.
>
> RITA
>
> Like who?

He shrugs.

Shift from film to video on DES.

> RITA *(V.O.)*
>
> How does your mom feel when you give her a
> present?
>
> DES
>
> Good.
>
> RITA *(V.O.)*
>
> You like it when she feels like that?
>
> DES
>
> Uh huh.

RITA *(V.O.)*
What does she do when she feels good?

DES
She smiles.

RITA
Oh yeah?

DES
Yeah.

Freeze frame: On DES. The video rewinds and plays again:

78. Interior. Rita's Office. Night. One Week Later.

RITA, smoking, is watching DES on tape, intently taking notes. The stack of videos has grown into a mini-mountain.

RITA *(V.O.)*
How does your Mom feel when you give her a present?

DES
Good.

RITA *(V.O.)*
You like it when she feels like that?

DES
Uh huh.

RITA *(V.O.)*
What does she do when she feels good?

DES
She smiles.

RITA *(V.O.)*
Oh yeah?

DES
Yeah ... She smiles at me ... You got a boy-friend?

RITA *(V.O.)*
Just one. My husband.

79. Exterior. Field Behind Children's House. Day.

Kids are playing ball in the field. Chasing, running, laughing. DES is by himself, on a bicycle, slowly riding it around the track beside the fence. RITA, smoking a cigarette, ponders DES from her window. LAURA joins her.

> LAURA:
> Can I talk to you for a minute?

80. Interior. Children's House/Des's Room. Day.

RITA and LAURA enter the empty room.

> LAURA:
> Mitch noticed that Des had been stealing pencils.

> RITA
> And?

> LAURA:
> He found this.

LAURA opens the closet door. RITA gapes. The walls of the closet are covered in DES's drawings. Endless and intricate pencil renderings of monkeys, severed hands, futuristic war machines, lions, skulls, vipers and beautiful flowers ...

81. Interior. Children's House/Rita's Office. Day.

DES looks at the table. Blank paper the drawing pencils.

> DES
> What's this?

> RITA
> ... I thought we'd try something different today.

> DES
> Like what?

> RITA
> I'd like you to draw something.

> DES
> I don't know how.

RITA
… Sure you do.

DES
Who says?

RITA
Draw anything. Anything you want.

DES takes a pencil and makes one swipe across the page. Stops.

RITA
Come on, Des, I know you can do better than
that.

*DES looks at her accusingly. RITA blanches as he searches her
face. She knows she's blown it. Too soon. Then he picks up the
pencil and violently crosses lines, making a disturbing, thick black
web.*

RITA
What're all these lines, Des?

*DES is silent. Then he makes a small red dot in the middle of the
morass.*

RITA
What is that?

DES
What do you care.

*He furiously draws through the paper ripping it, again and again.
RITA watches, her heart sinking.*

82. Interior. Des's Room/Children's House. Day.

*RITA opens DES's closet door. She gapes, horrified. DES's closet
has been completely trashed. The drawings scraped, covered with
mud and ink. RITA turns to leave but sees DES. He stares at RITA
defiantly.*

83. Interior. Children's House/Rita's Office. Day.

RITA
I'm sorry I was in your room, Des. I had no
right.

DES
Doesn't matter.

RITA

No. It does matter.

DES

Oh yeah?

RITA

I wish we had more time, Des.

DES

Sure.

RITA

Because your stay here will be finished soon.

DES

I don't mind staying.

RITA

Yeah, but this isn't a residence, Des. It's just an evaluation centre.

DES

So I could stay.

RITA

Well there's new kids coming in. There's just not enough space.

DES

Is it 'cause what I did to my room?

RITA

No. You had every right to be mad. You've been doing everything really well.

DES

I can't go back home.

RITA

That's alright, Des, you don't have to. We pulled some strings. Found you a really cool place.

DES

What kinda place?

RITA

The best foster home in the city.

DES

(ashen)

Foster home?

RITA

Yeah. Des, it's okay. I checked it all myself.
It's really great.

DES

I'm not going.

RITA

We don't have a choice.

DES

What did I do wrong?

RITA

(emphatic)

Nothing. You did nothing wrong, Des. You
gotta believe me.

DES stares at her, not believing it. Torn up.

RITA

Des?

DES looks lifeless. Not responding.

RITA

Des?

No response. He just stares blankly.

84. Exterior. The Field Behind Children's House. Day.

*DES is on a bicycle circling the bike track that runs along the
fence. His face is a mask as he circles again and again. Kids play
with a soccer ball in the field.*

85. Exterior. Children's House/The Fence. Day.

*The field is empty, the other kids gone, but DES still numbly pedals
the bike.*

CORY

Hey! Des, over here.

*DES stops and looks. CORY's on the other side of the fence. DES
doesn't react.*

CORY

Hey, look, it's me, man!

DES drops the bike and numbly moves towards him.

>   CORY
> Howya doin'?
>   DES
>   'Kay.
>   CORY
> Weird place, eh?
>   DES
>   Sucks.
>   CORY
>   So you comin'?

DES blankly stares at CORY. He doesn't move.

>   CORY
>   Hey, come on, man, We gotta blow!

DES snaps out of his paralysis. Looks at the facility that betrayed him.

>   CORY
>   Unless you'd rather stay here.
>   DES
>   Yeah, right!

DES hops the fence. And starts to run.

>   CORY
>   Hey, wait up, man!

DES, as he runs, in a fever, through the field to the street. Possessed. CORY, laughing, can barely keep up.

>   CORY
>   You crazy?

86. Exterior. The Docks. Day.

A match flares as CORY lights a joint and passes it to DES.

>   DES
>   I can't go back.
>   CORY
>   What're you talkin' about?
>   DES
>   They're puttin' me in a foster home.

CORY
No way. We'll just take off.

DES
Where?

CORY
Who cares, Vince and my mom got me grounded so bad it's like jail. Been locked up for three weeks and I'm sick of it. Took off school at lunch today and I'm not goin' back. I want out.

DES
You got cash?

CORY
No. But we know somebody who does.

DES
Like who?

CORY
Chet's always flush.

CORY pulls out DES's gun.

CORY
(continuing)
Picked it up from your place last night.

DES
Still works?

CORY
I don't know. Let's try it. Hey, Chet! *(fires it)* That's what you do, right? Wave it at him. He shits his pants. We take his money. Payback.

CORY notices DES's faraway expression.

CORY
... What's with you, you a droid or what?

CORY gives him the gun, trying to pump DES up.

CORY
Come on, man, we're the best. Nothing stops us!

CORY notices DES's arm.

> CORY
>
> What happened to your 'too?
>
> DES
>
> Got infected.
>
> CORY
>
> That sucks.

DES pockets the gun.

> DES
>
> Life sucks. Let's kick.

87. Exterior. Chet's House. Day.

CORY and DES run up Chet's steps. CORY pounds on the door. It opens.

> CHET
>
> Well, well, well. Look who's here.
>
> CORY
>
> You figure out who ripped the camera we sold you?
>
> CHET
>
> I'm on the case.
>
> CORY
>
> Check the jacket.

CORY shows off the tear. CHET looks.

> CHET
>
> What do you know? We got a perfect match here, Cinderella. So you gonna tell me what this is all about? Is this kiss and make up time— you want to make some kind of deal with me?
>
> CORY
>
> Yeah, that's it.
>
> CHET
>
> Sure, that's it, yeah …

CHET instantly grabs CORY and pulls him inside. DES, frozen in the threshold, watches.

88. Interior. The House. Day. Continuing.

CHET goes to CORY, collars him, jamming the boy against the wall.

CORY

Help me, Des.

But DES doesn't move.

CHET

You got something for me, Des? Huh, huh?

CORY

Help me, Des. Des!

CHET
(mocking)
Help me, Des! C'mon, help me, Des! ... Some
backup. You bunch of faggots.

He shoves CORY into the wall again. Turns. CHET freezes, gripping CORY by the shirt. DES is pointing the gun at him.

CHET

What are you doing ? Are you gonna shoot that
thing?

*DES, an automaton, releases the safety. CHET, frightened, frees
the battered CORY. He faces DES, palms open.*

CHET

Everything's cool, man! Just relax, okay? Just
relax, everything's fine!

CORY

Give us your money, jerkoff.

CHET

You want money, no problem. I got some right
here.

He starts to move cautiously to his wallet.

CORY

I'll get it.

CHET

Okay.

CORY moves. Picks up the wallet. Slaps CHET on the head.

> CORY
> Goof!
> *(to DES)*
> Took you long enough, man.

DES looks at him. CORY shows DES the stash.

> CORY
> Hey! Check this! We are happenin'!

DES smiles.

> CORY
> Let's boot!

CORY heads for the door.

> DES
> History.

DES fires the gun. CHET holds his bloody shoulder, amazed.

> CORY
> What're you doin!

Hearing the words, DES turns with the gun pointed at CORY.

> CORY
> Don't do it. Please.

DES blankly looks at him. Then turns back to CHET and fires. CHET hits the floor. CORY stares at DES, shocked, terrified. Drops the wallet. And runs like hell. In a cloud, DES watches him go. Looks at the dying CHET. Then walks slowly away.

89. Interior. Cory's Room. Day.

CORY is in bed, staring at the ceiling. Looks pale and afraid. Hasn't slept, fearful that he's DES's next victim. JUDY pushes open CORY's door.

> JUDY
> Aren't you up yet?

CORY's lying in bed, looking green.

> JUDY
> You better start moving. School.

> CORY
> I can't go.

JUDY
Oh Cory! Don't start playing games.

CORY
I'm sick.

JUDY feels his forehead. VINCE comes in. They share a look.

VINCE
Cory, you know the rules.

CORY
I don't feel good.

VINCE
We both know there's nothing wrong with you.

JUDY
... Cory, is it something else?

CORY looks at her, desperate to say something, but afraid to incriminate himself.

CORY
... No.

JUDY
You in some kind of trouble at school?

CORY
(shrugging it off)
No. No way.

VINCE
(to JUDY)
So?

JUDY
Still feel crummy after school, we'll take you
to the doctor.

CORY's heart sinks.

VINCE
The truck's leaving in ten minutes. Move.

90. Exterior. School Playground. Day.

DES walks through the playground, looking. MOUSE follows him.

DES
Did you see him?

MOUSE
No way. What d'ya want him for, Des?

DES
I just want him.

MOUSE
He's not here yet. His dad drops him off. I can
show you where.

DES
I know where.

91. Interior/Exterior. Truck. Day. Moving.

*VINCE irritably drives the newly repaired truck. CORY thinks he's
being taken to his own execution.*

VINCE
You've been doing just fine till this morning.
What's going on?

CORY
Nothin'. It's just today. I can't go today.

VINCE
What is it, you got a test in math?

CORY
Screw you.

VINCE
You know what, Cory? Screw you. You're in a
box. You made it, you live in it.

VINCE pulls up to the front of the school.

VINCE
Go on, get out.

CORY doesn't move.

VINCE
Move it. I'm outta here.

*But CORY doesn't respond. VINCE sees where CORY's looking.
DES is standing near the steps. Looking grimly determined.*

VINCE
I thought he was put away.

CORY

He was.

VINCE

You must be happy then, you'll have something to do today, get yourselves killed. Go on,
he's waiting. Just get the hell out.

*But CORY's frozen with fear. DES slowly moves closer. It hits
VINCE.*

VINCE

... What's going on, Cory?

CORY

Nuthin'.

VINCE

Talk to me.

CORY

I can't.

VINCE

Try.

Long silence.

CORY

... Don't make me ... go out there.

VINCE

Why?

CORY

Please.

VINCE searches CORY's face.

VINCE

... Okay. Okay.

CORY

Vince—

VINCE

You just stay here with me.

CORY

Lock the doors.

VINCE does.

VINCE
You're safe now, alright?

CORY
I don't think so. I was there.

CORY looks out at DES.

92. Exterior. Front of School. Day. Continuing.

DES watches the truck.

CORY looks at VINCE, completely vulnerable. VINCE puts his hand on CORY's shoulder. CORY starts pouring his heart out to VINCE.

From behind, CONSTABLE CLARKE approaches DES. Puts his hand on DES's shoulder. DES betrays nothing.

CLARKE
The running's over, son. People try to help
you, I try to help you, but nothing changes.

The truck starts to back away.

DES
Lemmee go!

CLARKE
You're with me till the social worker comes to
pick you up.

DES
No!

DES struggles and breaks away. Runs. CLARKE starts to chase him, stops.

CLARKE
Hey Des, May Twenty-Ninth!

DES, from a distance, stops.

CLARKE
Your mom gave us the date on the form. You're
twelve next month. Happy Birthday, Pal.

CLARKE glumly watches him disappear around the corner.

93. Exterior. Des's House/Street. Day.

*DES runs down the empty grey streets. Comes to his house. Makes
a break for the basement window. Crawls in.*

94. Interior. House/Hallway. Day.

*The basement door quietly opens. DES furtively listens for any
sound. Nothing. He moves toward the living room. Looks in. Nobody. He keeps moving.*

95. Interior. Ruth's Bedroom.

*DES carefully steps into the room. RUTH is there, passed out on
the bed with a rough looking man.*

DES stealthily heads to her side of the bed.

>DES
>Mom ... Mom ...

>RUTH
>... I'm sleepin'.

>DES
>Mom, it's me ...

*She opens a blurry eye. Looks at him. Touches his head. She turns
over and is back asleep. DES stares for a second, then heads out.*

96. Interior. Kitchen. Day.

*A match ignites. DES throws it into the sink, dishes piled high. A
cockroach ducks for cover. DES sits at the table with a box of
kitchen matches. He lights another, flicks it into the sink. Another.
Another. One hits the curtain. It slowly starts to burn. DES leaves
the room, ignoring the smoke.*

97. Interior. Stairs. Day. Continuing.

*DES, almost in a trance, moves up the stairs. Behind him, smoke is
beginning to waft out the kitchen door.*

98. Interior. Des's Bedroom. Day. Continuing.

DES opens the closet door and goes inside.

99. Interior. House. Stairway.

The flames have reached the bannister, licking their way up the stairs. The walls are blistering, the paint peeling from the heat.

100. Interior. Des's Closet. Day.

DES turns on a big drycell flashlight. With a pen knife, he pulls up a floorboard. Lifts out the old metal box. Opens it. He puts the revolver inside. Takes out some marking pens. Starts to draw a monkey on the closet walls. In the background, sirens wail. He yawns. Puts down the markers. As his eyes close, his thumb slips into his mouth. The smoke slowly filters in from the crack of light at the bottom of the door.

> RITA *(V.O.)*
> 'So you went back to get Nonny's monkey?

> DES *(V.O.)*
> Yeah.

Dissolve to:

101. Interior. Children's House/Rita's Office. Day.

RITA, red-eyed, strikes a match. It flares. She lights her cigarette. And stares at DES in close up on the monitor.

> RITA *(off-screen)*:
> Why?

> DES
> She was crying and stuff. Like she wanted it bad, right?

> RITA *(off-screen)*:
> Did Cory want to get it?

> DES
> No. He was afraid of getting caught. I made him come.

> RITA *(off-screen)*:
> Did you find it?

> DES
> Yeah. It was in the closet.

RITA *(off-screen)*:
That was a very nice thing to do, Des.

DES
She was crying really bad.

RITA *(off-screen)*:
What did hearing her cry make you feel like?

DES
Bad, I guess.

RITA *(off-screen)*:
Ever feel that way before?

DES
… I don't remember.

The image of DES freezes on the monitor, staring at us. It lingers on the screen, flickering.

Fade out.
The end.

Original Storyboards

A number of Kelly Brine's original storyboard sketches are included here both to help the reader visualize the film and to better understand the production process. Storyboards for scenes three, four, twenty-eight and forty are included.

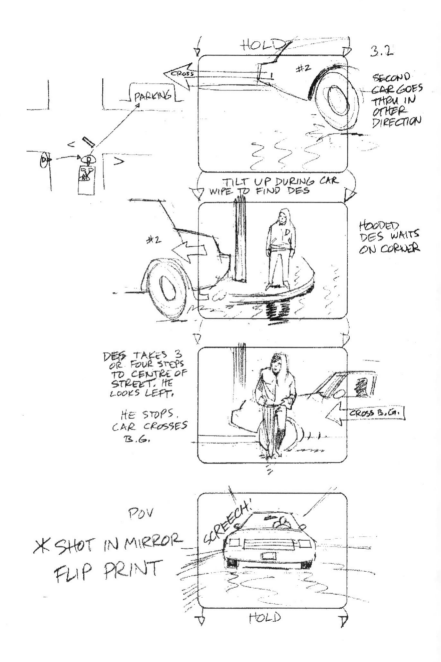

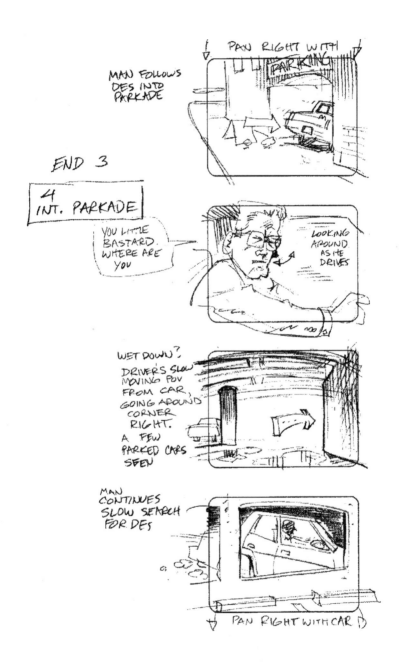

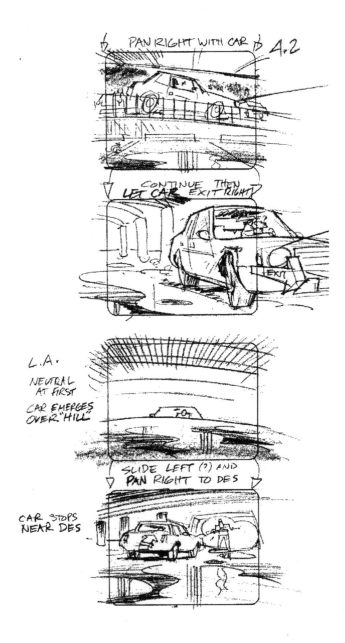

PAN RIGHT WITH CAR 4.2

CONTINUE THEN LET CAR EXIT RIGHT

EXIT

L.A.
NEUTRAL AT FIRST
CAR EMERGES OVER "HILL"

SLIDE LEFT (?) AND PAN RIGHT TO DES

CAR STOPS NEAR DES

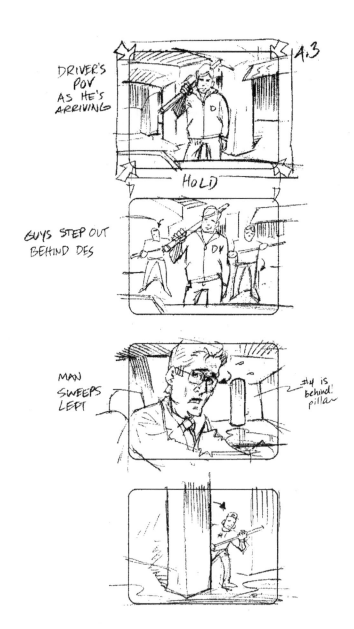

DRIVER'S
POV
AS HE'S
ARRIVING

HOLD

GUYS STEP OUT
BEHIND DES

MAN
SWEEPS
LEFT

A.3

#4 is
behind!
pillar

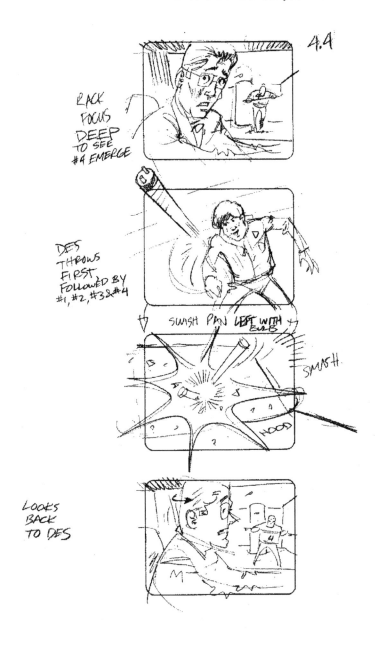

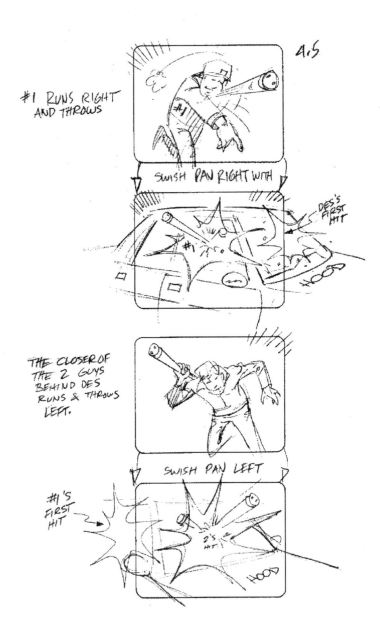

#1 RUNS RIGHT AND THROWS

4.5

SWISH PAN RIGHT WITH

DES'S FIRST HIT

THE CLOSER OF THE 2 GUYS BEHIND DES RUNS & THROWS LEFT.

SWISH PAN LEFT

#1'S FIRST HIT

2'S HIT

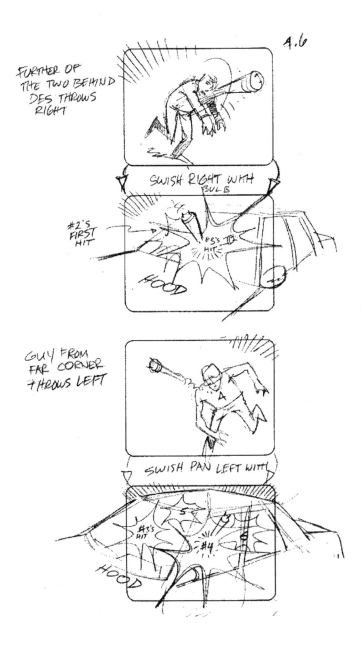

4.6

FURTHER OF
THE TWO BEHIND
DES THROWS
RIGHT

SWISH RIGHT WITH
BULB

#2'S
FIRST
HIT

#3'S
HIT

HOOD

GUY FROM
FAR CORNER
+ THROWS LEFT

SWISH PAN LEFT WITH

#3'S
HIT

#4

HOOD

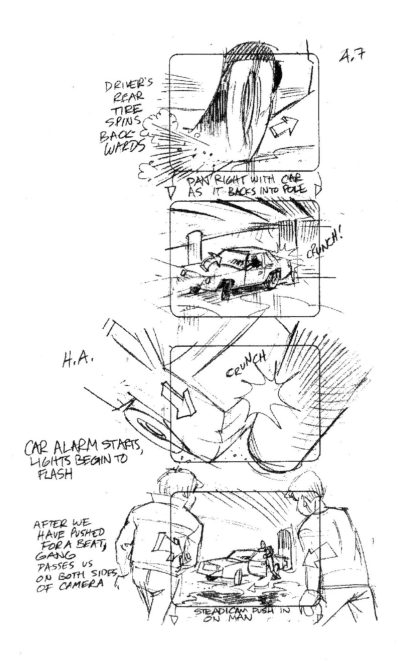

4.7

DRIVER'S
REAR
TIRE
SPINS
BACK-
WARDS

PAN RIGHT WITH CAR
AS IT BACKS INTO POLE

CRUNCH!

H.A.

CRUNCH

CAR ALARM STARTS,
LIGHTS BEGIN TO
FLASH

AFTER WE
HAVE PUSHED
FOR A BEAT,
GANG
PASSES US
ON BOTH SIDES
OF CAMERA

STEADICAM PUSH IN
ON MAN

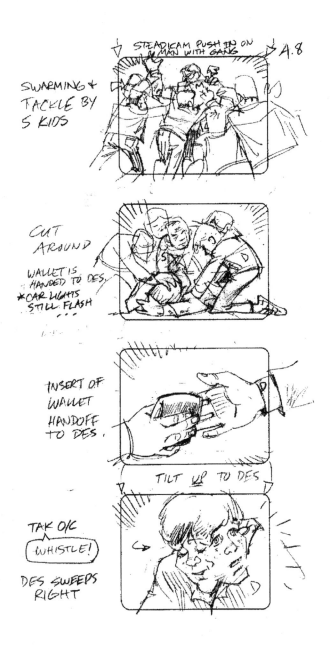

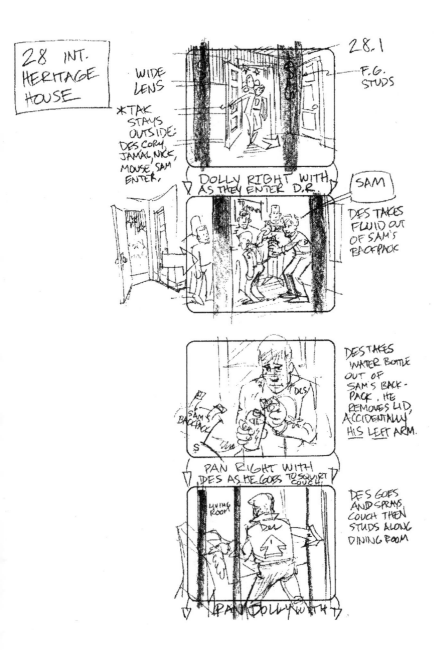

28 INT. HERITAGE HOUSE

28.1

WIDE LENS

*TAK STAYS OUTSIDE: DES CORY, JAMAL, NICK, MOUSE, SAM ENTER.

F.G. STUDS

DOLLY RIGHT WITH AS THEY ENTER D.R.

SAM

DES TAKES FLUID OUT OF SAM'S BACKPACK

SAM'S BACKPACK

DES TAKES WATER BOTTLE OUT OF SAM'S BACKPACK. HE REMOVES LID, ACCIDENTALLY HIS LEFT ARM.

PAN RIGHT WITH DES AS HE GOES TO SQUIRT COUCH.

DES GOES AND SPRAYS COUCH THEN STUDS ALONG DINING ROOM

LIVING ROOM

PAN DOLLY WITH

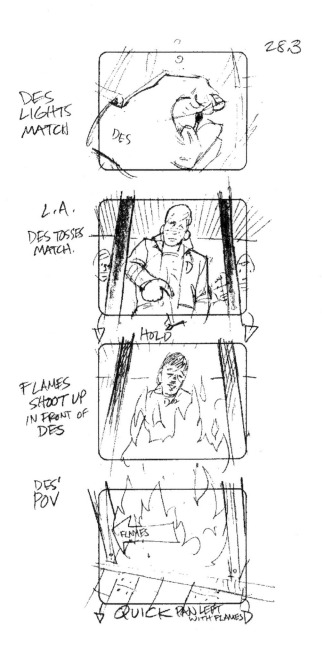

28.3

DES
LIGHTS
MATCH

DES

L.A.

DES TOSSES
MATCH.

HOLD

FLAMES
SHOOT UP
IN FRONT OF
DES

DES'
POV

FLAMES

QUICK PAN LEFT
WITH FLAMES

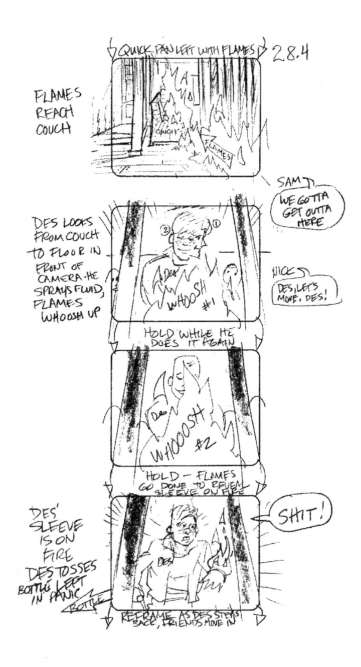

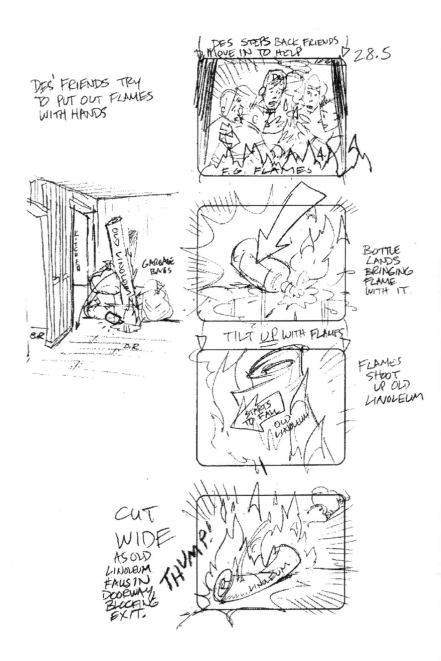

DES' FRIENDS TRY TO PUT OUT FLAMES WITH HANDS

DES STEPS BACK FRIENDS MOVE IN TO HELP

28.5

D

C

F.G. FLAMES

KITCHEN

OLD LINOLEUM

GARBAGE BAGS

B.R.

D.R.

BOTTLE LANDS BRINGING FLAME WITH IT.

TILT UP WITH FLAMES

STARTS TO FALL

OLD LINOLEUM

FLAMES SHOOT UP OLD LINOLEUM

CUT WIDE AS OLD LINOLEUM FALLS IN DOORWAY BLOCKING EXIT.

THUMP!

LINOLEUM

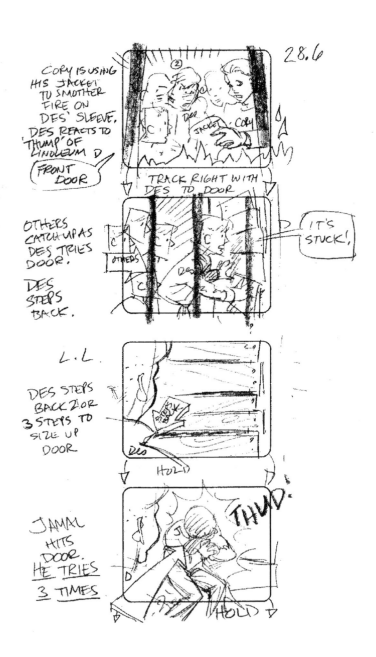

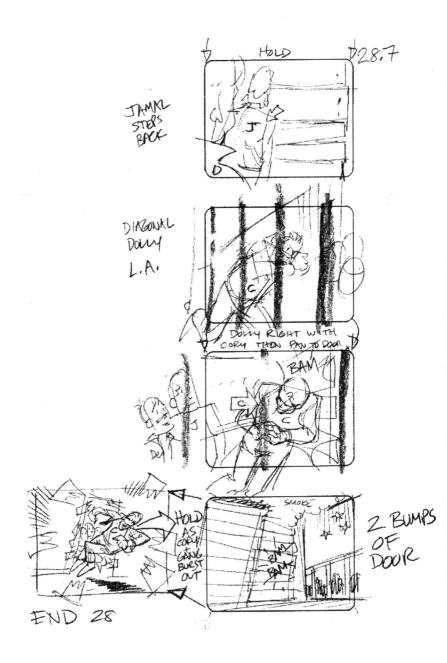

Credits

Des	Brendan Fletcher
Cory	Myles Ferguson
Mouse	Adam Harrison
Nick	John Nguyen
Jamal	London Sam-Baergen
Sam	Jordon Clarke
Tak	Loc Vo
Rita	Mimi Kuzyk
Vince	Randy Hughson
Chet	Jed Rees
Ruth	Sabrina Grdevich
Judy	Sonia Norris
Clarke	Dwight McFee
Kostash	Callum Rennie
Nonny	Keely Purvis
Social Worker	Molly Parker
Constable	Winston Brown
Dolly	Dolores Drake
Nurse	Elizabeth Dancoes
Mitch	Andrew Kavadas
Hospital Nurse	Kamilyn Kaneko
Driver	Terry King
Saleslady	Betty Linde
Teacher	Joyce Erickson
Tattoo Artist	Percy Lemaigre
Dink	Joshua Simeon
Stacker	Beeshu "B.J." Wawrzasek
Security Guard	Brett Armstrong
Josh	Aaron Goff
Little Joe	Massimo Cusano

Directed by Stephen Surjik

Produced by Phil Savath

Executive in charge of Production
Brian Freeman

Creative Head Movies and Miniseries
Jim Burt

Production Executive
Dee Gilchrist

Head of Talent
Maria Armstrong

Line Producer
Barbara Kelly

Director of Photography
Stephen Reizes

Edited by Alison Grace

Music Score by Fred Mollin

Costume Designer
Karen Matthews

Production Designer
Lawrence Collett

Casting by
Sid Kozak

Production Manager
Don McLean

First Assistant Director
Alex Pappas

Music Supervisor
Fred Mollin

Production Coordinator
Erica Maletz

Post Production Supervisor
Brenda Longland

Music Clearance
Peter Coquillard .

First Assistant Editor
Michelle Floyd

Script Supervisor
Janet Munro

Unit Manager
Jacquie Fitzgerald

Assistant Production Coordinator
Cathy Parke

Production Assistants
Mark Overgaard
Kimberley Wakefiled

Assistant to Stephen Surjik
Brendan Ferguson

Accountants
Laureen Hui
Serafina Crawley
Gale Bourne
Ralph Motohashi

Second Assistant Director
Lawrence Jones

Third Assistant Director
Arlene Arnold

Trainee Assistant Director
Velma Roberts

Dialogue Coach
Sherry Bie

Set Counsellor
Jennifer Newman

Police Consultant
Mark Lalonde

Children's Tutor
Jean Armes

Children's Coordinator
Stephanie Miller

Storyboard Artist
Kelly Brine

Location Manager
John Penhall

Location Production Assistants
David Ray
Mark Kandborg
Jennifer McLean

Art Director
Peter Hinton

Set Decorator
David Birdsall

Assistant Set Decorator
Anne Power

Set Buyer
Darryl Deegan

Set Dressers
All Berardo
Christian Rondow
Files Bobic

Property Master
Brent Lane

Assistant Props
Trinita Waller

Perparation Costumer
Jana MacDonald

Set Costumer
Gail Smith

Set Costumer
Janice Devries

Seamstress
Nora Bautista

Makeup Artist
Jacky Wilkinson

Assistant Makeup
Katie Bentley

Hari Stylist
Sherry Anne Ross

Assistant Hair
Adina Hawkes

Camera Operator
Neil Seale

Focus Puller
Bill St. John

Second Camera Assistant
Norine Mark

Camera Trainee
Carol Campbell

Video Playback
Klaus Melchoir
Rob Parisienne

Stills Photographer
Philip Hersee

Sound Mixer
Hans Fousek

Boom Operator
Bill Moore

Key Grip
Ken Hemphill

Best Boy
John Baxter

Dolly Grip
Al White

Grips
Bill Wouterloot
John O'Neill

Gaffer
Amir Mohammed

Best Boy
Rob Weber

Lamp Operator
Peter Lyew

Genny Operator
Ron "Rocky Cairns

Special Effects Coordinator
John Sleep

Special Effects Consultant
Gary Paller

Special Effects Assistant
Dave Paller

Stunt Coordinator
Bill Ferguson

Construction Coordinator
Mike Rennison

Construction Foreman
Paul Renaldi

Lead Carpenter
Adrian Dowell

Scene Carpenters
Chris Gamel
Rick Willoughby

Carpenter
Mike Richardson

Lead Labourer
Marlow Pederson

Labourer
Sean Wynia

Head Painter
Jenny Seinen

Lead Hand
Eileen Telfer Rennick

Scenic Painterr
James Blake
Brian Wadsworth

Plasterer
Michael Raycevick

Casting Assistant
Amber Woodward

Extras Casting
Andrea Brown

Trnasportation Coordinator
Mark Gould

Transportation Captain
Ross "Grizz" Wilkinson

Co-Captain
Rick Cavazzi

Drivers
Dave MacDonald
Dave Brownlee
Scott Delaplace

Security
Gerry Baker

Craft Service
Sherry Rounds-Popoff
Karen Popoff

Publicity
Jennifer Young
Ginny Belwood

Gastown Post
Flavio Bidese
Janice Cotter
Angela Stevenson

Titles Design
Eclipse – Vancouver

Assitant Music Clearance
Tom Eaton

Adio Post Production
Sharpe Sound Studios Inc.

Sound Supervisor
Jacqueline Christianini

Sound Editors
Anke Bakker
Sheena Macrae
Sophie Hotte

Foley Recordist
Don Painchaud

Foley Artists
Cam Wagner
Shane Shemko

Group Walla
John Pantges & the Background
Walla Recordists
Bill Mellow

Re-Recording Mixers
Paul A. Sharpe
Dean Giammarco

Special Thanks to:
Tammy and Rick Johns
Susan Duligal
Theresa Goode
Toronto Blue Jays
Delaney and Friends
Echo Toys Limited
Kurzweil Music Systems – Young Chang Pianos
and Jackson/Charvel and Godin Guitars

"Violet"
Performed by Hole
Courtesy of DGC Records

"Groove Stew"
Performed by Tom Waits
Courtesy of Island Records, Inc.
By arrangement with Polygram Film and TV Licensing

"It's All Over"
Performed by the Headstones
Courtesy of MCA Records Canada

"Smoke 'Em If You Got 'Em"
Performed by the Hungary Crocodiles
Courtesy of Windswept Pacific

"Crimson and Clover"
Performed by Tommy James and the Shondells
Courtesy of Rhino Records
By arrangement with Warner Special Products

"Roads"
Performed by Portishead
Courtesy of Go!Disc/London Records
By arrangement with Polygram Film and TV Licensing

"Creep"
Performed by Radiohead
Courtesy of Capitol Records
Under License from CEMA Special Markets